DEFEATING
TERROR

DEFEATING TERROR

BEHIND THE HUNT FOR THE BALI BOMBERS

DAVID CRAIG
FORMER AUSTRALIAN FEDERAL POLICE AGENT

hardie grant books

Published in 2017 by Hardie Grant Books

Hardie Grant Books (Australia)
Ground Floor, Building 1
658 Church Street
Richmond, Victoria 3121
www.hardiegrant.com.au

Hardie Grant Books (UK)
5th & 6th Floors
52–54 Southwark Street
London SE1 1UN
www.hardiegrant.co.uk

All rights reserved. No part of this publication may be reproduced, stored in a retrieval system or transmitted in any form by any means, electronic, mechanical, photocopying, recording or otherwise, without the prior written permission of the publishers and copyright holders.

The moral rights of the author have been asserted.

Copyright text © David Craig 2017

A Cataloguing-in-Publication entry is available from the catalogue of the National Library of Australia at www.nla.gov.au

Defeating Terror
ISBN 978 1 74379 330 5

Cover design by Luke Causby/Blue Cork
Front cover image courtesy Getty Images
Typeset in Bembo by Kirby Jones
Printed in Australia by McPherson's Printing Group, Maryborough, Victoria

The paper this book is printed on is certified against the Forest Stewardship Council® Standards. FSC promotes environmentally responsible, socially beneficial and economically viable management of the world's forests.

**To the victims of terror and those
with the courage to counter it.**

Evil manifests; not in the text,
but in the teaching.

CONTENTS

Foreword   1

PART ONE – A doctor's radicalisation   **3**

Bali, bloody Bali Two   5

Naked   17

Who the hell is Jamaah Islamiyah?   25

Wiring the Islamic kill-switch   34

A fertile field   42

Ripe fruit   52

MILF   63

Meanwhile, back in Australia ...   72

PART TWO – The evolution of killing   **81**

A critical mass   83

No place for family   93

Jimi's cake   100

Big fish   114

The unnamed   123

Unleashed   130

Sharia law & holy war   139

The wedding planners   147

PART THREE – The sin of Bin	**163**
Brain taser	165
The plot	179
Heads, you win	183
Anthrax & flowers	193
Long shots	203
Batu silence	220
A Muslim and two Christians walk into a bar	232
Aftermath	236
Ever	239
Main players	249
Main events	253
Endnotes	254

FOREWORD

For over 22 years, I had the privilege of being an Australian Federal Police (AFP) officer. For the last 10 years, I was a detective superintendent serving both in Australia and overseas. Those roles provided me with access to privileged and highly classified information. There are very strict laws surrounding disclosure of such information to which I remain legally bound. I have changed some names and some circumstances to allow me to share with you as close to the truth as is legally possible. Some changes were also required to protect the identity and security of some Indonesian interviewees, witnesses and police, who may be targeted by Jamaah Islamiyah for providing information. Where changes have been made, they remain highly indicative of what really occurred.

There were, and are, dozens of Islamic terrorist splinter groups throughout Southeast Asia, one of which is Jamaah Islamiyah, the group that radicalised Azhari bin Husin (Azhari), the technical mastermind behind the Bali bombings. This book focuses predominantly on Azhari and his radicalisation, so some terrorist figures and organisations have been excluded.

This book is about terrorism and my experience with it. It doesn't dress up the ugly reality of the subject, nor does it hide the complicity and complacency of those who silently or actively support its goals. Just as a book written about police corruption focuses upon corrupt police, not the majority of honest officers, this book focuses on Islamic terrorists, not the majority of peaceful Muslims. This book does not criticise Islam, but the terrorists who commit atrocities in its name.

This is a small glimpse into the abhorrent truth about Islamic terrorism in Southeast Asia and how otherwise good people can be radicalised. It's also an inspirational story for moderate Muslims and the broader community: that, together, can we thwart the scourge that misuses Islam as an excuse for cowardly murder.

PART ONE

A DOCTOR'S RADICALISATION

BALI, BLOODY BALI TWO

1 October 2005

It's a typically warm and sunny day in Kuta, Bali. There's a balmy offshore breeze flapping the colourful flags on the white masts of outriggers strategically positioned above the high-water mark. There's a menagerie of beachgoers, some surfing, some swimming, and some laying on beach towels absorbing every ray the Indonesian sun delivers to their oiled bodies.

Punctuating the beach crowd are the unmistakable blue conical hats covering the heads of the local women who tirelessly massage grateful tourists lying prone on grass beach mats. Seasoned massagees fend off circulating groups of young Indonesians and decline their offers of simultaneous hair braiding, pedicures and T-shirt sales; others succumb to the good-natured haranguing.

In the surrounding streets, tourists run the retail gauntlet of relentless street hawkers and stallholders. Some travellers seek shelter in the shade of Balinese bamboo and brick-structured bars and cafes where they crack a cold beverage and share their holiday experiences.

This is Bali – the holiday home away from home for thousands of Aussies.

It's almost three years since the 2002 bombings killed 202 people, including 88 Australians. The chaos and carnage of that night has faded in the minds of many. But most visitors will, at some stage, visit the Bali Bombing Memorial to pause and remember. Two days ago, Terry Fitzgerald, a 43-year-old real estate agent from Western Australia, did just that with his son Brendan (age 16), a talented footballer, and his daughter Jessica (age 13). While there, they searched the list of deceased Australians until they found Carol Johnstone, the name of one of Brendan's teachers from Busselton. The small family group shared a thoughtful moment for the victims – unaware they would be next.

What the Fitzgeralds didn't know that day was that a small group of fanatical Muslim men with murder on their minds had just arrived in Bali. It had been months in the planning and Australians were firmly in their crosshairs.

About 2.20 pm, the men negotiate their way by motor scooter through the chaotic streets to the resplendent beachfront Hard Rock Cafe, in time for afternoon prayers. They enter the beach between the two towering concrete Hindu sculptures placed there to welcome visitors to the beach. Beside one of the sculptures is a small white concrete building, the base for an incongruously placed orange-and-white television transmission tower. The trio lurk behind the building, out of sight from the hundreds of people enjoying the beach, until it is time for Asr prayers. At 2.40 pm, each man kneels next to his explosives-filled backpack and commences praying.

Just then, having left their accommodation next to the Hard Rock Cafe moments earlier, Terry and Brendan Fitzgerald walk along the beach path on the other side of the building, chatting on the way to their first and, as fate would have it, last surfing session together.

Jessica Fitzgerald has a mild case of Bali belly and is resting in the hotel room while Terry and Brendan sit on their boards, just beyond the breaking waves. The orange-flooded sky is fading slowly as the sun starts to sink toward the warm tropical waters. A set of solid swells silently rolls its way in from the open ocean. The flock of keen surfers reacts and starts to jockey for a position in readiness. Terry paddles hard and catches the wave. He takes the drop and sets himself a course to carve the unbroken bank when another surfer drops in on him. It's then that Terry realises the offending surfer is

DEFEATING TERROR

Brendan. At that moment, time freezes in Terry's mind. He would later write,

> I thought then that this was a very special moment, father and son riding the same wave while on holiday. I thought that, in years to come, Brendan and I would reflect on that moment. Little did I know just how special that moment was to become.[1]

While the Aussie father and son are surfing, the terrorist trio complete their prayers then conduct reconnaissance on Raja's Bar and Restaurant in Kuta Square before returning to their boarding house. There they wait.

About 5.10 pm, earlier than instructed, they carefully pack their belongings, including their respective copies of the attack plan, into their backpacks so everything will be destroyed in the explosion, leaving no trace for the police.

The plan is for them to conduct Maghrib (evening prayer time) on the beach and then proceed immediately to their allocated targets. Like other Islamic prayer times, Maghrib is timed on the position of the sun; today it's at 6.17 pm, immediately after sunset. However, their early departure has them returning to the beach in front of the Hard Rock Cafe way too early.

Either to avoid suspiciously loitering in the area, or to conduct one last reconnaissance of Raja's, the three men leave

8

the area on foot. In the fading light, the men walk purposefully along the beachfront and turn towards Kuta Square. Any fear or anxiety would have been extinguished by their hate-filled sense of duty and the expectation of eternal paradise that martyrdom would deliver.

As they reach the street corner near Raja's, they unexpectedly come face-to-face with the Jamaah Islamiyah (JI) attack commander. He's an unassuming middle-aged Asian man with circular John Lennon-style glasses. His attack plan has been timed to the second, so his usual quiet demeanour is immediately replaced with rage when he sees the three men near Raja's well before the scheduled time. He gesticulates angrily as the three men huddle around him like naughty schoolchildren.

At that precise time, Terry, Brendan and Jessica are shopping in Kuta Square. Terry notices the group of men on the corner. It strikes him that they appear to be very serious, not the usual jovial laid-back Balinese he was used to seeing. He thinks they may be up to no good or are perhaps just angry about something; a terrorist attack doesn't cross his mind.[2] Even if it had, what could he or anyone else have done? If anyone interfered with the group, they simply would have detonated themselves instantly. Nothing was going to stop this murderous freight train.

The commander inspects the left shoulder strap of each man's backpack and is satisfied when he sees the small green

LED hidden just underneath the woven material, shining through its tiny pinhole. The bombs are primed and ready. He dismisses the men who then walk back to the beach to wait for prayer time.

Just before 7 pm, Terry, Brendan and Jessica Fitzgerald have finished their shopping and are looking for a place for dinner. After looking at several restaurants along the shopping strip, they innocently enter the multi-level Raja's Bar and Restaurant. Raja's, as usual, is bustling with the upbeat chatter of diners. Amongst the hubbub, tireless Balinese waiters ferry cold Bintangs and other drinks to the thirsty throng. The entire dining area is enveloped in an appetising grilled-satay fog.

The Fitzgeralds are guided to a table on the ground floor at the back of the restaurant. Terry sits with his back to the bar with a view out to the street. Brendan's on Terry's right, while Jessica sits directly opposite her father. At 7.41 pm they are considering Raja's menu options when one of the bombers walks quickly in from the street towards the back of the building where they are seated. Without breaking stride, the bomber scans the diners so he can position himself correctly. Just as he has been trained, he turns his back and faces the wall to direct the full force of the blast into the crowd.

He flicks the detonation switch. In that instant, all the oxygen is sucked from Terry's lungs towards the exploding backpack less than three metres away. This flow is then violently reversed by an entropic burst of explosive energy, instantaneously followed by a shower of red-hot shrapnel and a 1200-degree fireball. The bomber's head is torn through the neck and propelled in the blast wave that throws the three Australians and everyone else in its path across the room.

Then it's black.

Terry's breath has been replaced with searing hot ash and dust that fills his lungs and burns deep inside his chest. A large piece of wood has impaled his leg and the flesh on his badly burnt back is sticking to the white-tiled floor. Terry doesn't know where Jessica and Brendan are and can only move his head. He thinks everything is silent because both his eardrums have been ruptured – but around him is death, chaos and panic. Terry has caught most of the blast with his back, protecting Jessica from the full force of steel shrapnel rain. Brendan isn't so lucky; his body is drilled by hundreds of searing ball bearings.

Time once again freezes in Terry's mind. He will later recount, 'At some time, not long after the blast, Brendan came to me, all I could see was his face and shirt. He said, "Won't be picked for any more games, Dad."

'I said, "What?"

'He said, "I just won't be playing any more games," and he was gone.'[3]

*

DEFEATING TERROR

At Jimbaran Bay, just 10 kilometres from Raja's, but a world away from the murder and mayhem unfolding in Kuta, hundreds of tourists are enjoying alfresco dining at the numerous seafood restaurants nestled together along the Jimbaran Bay shorefront. The restaurants are constructed similarly, with concrete slab floors swept to a gloss by hardworking Indonesian staff. Large wooden poles support the thick thatched roofs that cover the few diners inside. Most visitors prefer to dine outside at one of the multitude of tables set up on the sandy strip of flat beach between the line of restaurant buildings and the quietly lapping waters of Jimbaran Bay.

Amongst the diners on this night is a group of 18 Australian parents from Newcastle who had coordinated their family trips to Bali so their sons, students from St Francis Xavier College, could spend a surfing holiday together – with parental supervision. They had arrived at the Nyoman restaurant in time to watch the volcanic orange sunset gently transition to a perfectly clear night sky carpeted with stars. Now, mimicking the stars, candles are gently flickering atop the several hundred dining tables set out along the beach.

The Newcastle group's conversations are punctuated with laughter as they converse around the long wooden dining table resting on the soft white sand. In contrast to the rest of the group is Aleta Lederwasch, a 21-year-old university student. She is seated with her mother, Julia, a teacher at the school, and her father, Dietmar. Unlike the rest of the group, Aleta feels uncomfortable. In fact, she'd felt on edge since she had arrived in Bali. With the media reports of the Bali 2002 bombings etched in her mind, it was difficult for her to shake an inexplicable feeling of impending danger.

That danger is now personified in the form of two Muslim terrorists who are lurking at a nearby street stall just beyond the reach of the street lighting.

Just 500 metres away from the diners, on an isolated bushy headland of Jimbaran Bay, a thin Indonesian man in his mid-twenties is sitting on a motor scooter nervously smoking a Gudang clove cigarette. His name is Muhammad Cholili. Next to Cholili is the bespectacled JI commander.

Some, including Cholili himself, will report, publicly at least, that neither the commander nor Cholili were there that night – but that's not what he'll tell me later.[4] The commander has a long history of watching the bombs he's designed and made explode. He revels in it. From their overwatch position at Jimbaran Bay they didn't get to watch or hear the Raja's attack, so the commander doesn't want to miss the glory of this one.

About 7.45 pm they watch intently as two familiar silhouettes carrying backpacks move from the food stalls on the street down onto the beach. They slink along the water's edge, one man 50 metres behind the other. Death is on its way.

DEFEATING TERROR

The commander is desperately hoping for Australian deaths. He knows Australia – he used to live there. To avoid confusion, he's instructed the men to look for white people, which they do as they approach the restaurant strip along the dark water's edge. The eyes of the second silhouette are focused on the 'white' group from Newcastle.

At 7.47 pm, just six minutes after the Raja's explosion, the first dark shape reaches an area adjacent to Menega Cafe. He looks behind and can see the shadowy figure of his old school friend almost in line with the Nyoman restaurant. Then he turns right and walks quickly into the centre of Menega Cafe and detonates the backpack. It sends a shower of shrapnel slicing into the flesh of innocent diners and staff. The bright orange fireball instantly floods the Menega dining area with light as its force throws people and furniture asunder.

The thunderous clap shakes the ground beneath the tables at the Nyoman restaurant. Someone at the Newcastle table, trying to remain calm, says, 'That must have been a gas bottle exploding.'

Aleta Lederwasch, though, doesn't need any second-guessing. Her natural fight–or–flight response instantly selects flight.

'I knew this would happen!' she yells as she pushes her chair back and then runs in the opposite direction to the Menega explosion.[5] Julia Lederwasch's mothering instinct hits overdrive

BALI, BLOODY BALI TWO

and she gives chase. Focused on catching her daughter, Julia doesn't notice as she runs past the second shape that is walking determinedly towards the Newcastle table.

Just as Julia catches up and embraces Aleta, the shape reaches the Newcastle table and yells *'Allahu Akbar!'* ('God is great'), detonating the contents of his backpack, sending a second wave of carnage and chaos throughout the restaurant strip. His head is immediately severed and propelled into the air before skidding along one of the tables, rolling off and landing in the sand that thirstily absorbs its fluids. There it rests like a macabre trophy as calamity reigns. Some traumatised witnesses will later mistakenly report they saw a bomb thrown along or under the table. There was no such bomb.

With each explosion, the commander and Cholili passionately yell *'Allahu Akbar'* in unison. After the second blast, they quickly don their dark-visored motorcycle helmets and motor away towards the Balinese port of Gilimanuk.

During the scant few minutes of the synchronised attacks, the three blasts kill 20 people, including Australians Brendan Fitzgerald, Jennifer Williamson, and Colin and Fiona Zwolinski, whose sons Ben and Isaac were resting in their Kuta hotel room, completely unaware they had just become orphans. Aleta Lederwasch suffers nonlethal shrapnel wounds, while her mother, Julia, sustains minor injuries and her father survives with barely a scratch. Aleta's instinctive actions most likely saved the pair; others at the Newcastle table weren't so lucky. The attack has also killed 15 Indonesians, one Japanese and injured over 120 others – and many more will have their lives tragically altered.[6]

While panic and pain spreads throughout Bali, Cholili and the commander cruise to a secluded beach area near Gilimanuk. There, it's likely a JI member or affiliate takes them on board an outrigger headed for Java.

Another clean getaway by the commander. In under five years, his organisation has killed or injured more than 1000 people.[7] His name is Azhari bin Husin. He's a doctor, but not one that saves lives – one that takes them.

NAKED

1 October 2005

While Azhari and Cholili were on the outrigger fleeing the crime scene that Bali had become once again, I was stepping into the shower at home in Cairns, North Queensland, where I had been posted by the Australian Federal Police (AFP). As a consequence of my rapid promotion, I had travelled a lot over the past few years and missed my wife and the kids greatly. The offer of a promotion to Detective Superintendent of North Queensland promised a hiatus from the constant travel and the hectic professional and academic pace I had set for myself.

Despite being Officer-in-Charge for AFP operations for about half of Queensland's coastline, with staff based in Cairns, Townsville and Thursday Island, my new role provided some much-needed routine and family stability – something we hadn't had for years. This was a happy period and I spent most nights at home. My wife and children loved it, and so did I.

On that evening I had no idea of what had just unfolded in Bali. I was a world away, listening to the Cockroaches, my favourite Australian band before their transformation into The Wiggles – who were now my children's favourite group. The bathroom CD player was pumping out, 'Hey! Let's go, let's go, let's go. Hey! Let's go, let's go, let's go.'

I closed my eyes. The song took me straight back to their concert a decade before. The lead singer, Paul Field, dripping in sweat, seeming to spend more time in the air than on the stage, somehow managing to keep up with the gritty guitar rhythms belted out by his brothers, Anthony and John. Jeff Fatt hitting the keyboard like a man possessed and Tony Henry on drums holding the band's energy in time, just.

While the refreshing flow of cool water washed away Cairns's tropical humidity, I mused that soon enough I'd be needing a hot shower to warm up, as was usually the case in Canberra. Five days earlier I had been contacted by AFP senior management and asked if I would be willing to fill in acting at a higher rank as Commander of Counterterrorism in Canberra.

I had led in a diverse variety of operational areas, counterterrorism *not* being one of them. In fact, it seemed as though I was one of the very few in the AFP that had not worked, at least in part, on the first Bali bombing investigation. All I knew about that was what I'd read in the Sunday papers. I'd enjoyed reading about the success of the Indonesian–Australian multinational task force that investigated JI and brought to justice those responsible for the bombing. To me then, Azhari was just a name – but he was soon to become much more than that.

I've never been one to shy away from risk, opportunity or hard work. Stepping in as the commander of all AFP counterterrorism investigations with no direct experience was a challenge ... but I'd taken on plenty of challenges in my time with the AFP, so I accepted the offer. I knew it would be a steep learning curve but it was only for two weeks; how hard could it be?

My wife slid open the bathroom door. 'David your phone is going crazy,' she said, holding the phone so I could see the screen.

'Twenty-three missed calls, twelve messages! I've only been in the shower for five minutes. How can that be?'

The answer was simple. Senior AFP management had asked me to start in Canberra on Monday 3 October 2005, when I would be introduced to the staff, interdepartmental contacts and be briefed on current counterterrorism operations. However, technically I had taken the reins at the start of the month: 1 October. As such, the IT system had automatically updated the emergency counterterrorism phone lists to have my name second from the top, under the Assistant Commissioner of Counterterrorism. As fate would have it, that assistant commissioner was travelling out of mobile phone range, and would be so for several hours, leaving me as the number one go-to contact for AFP counterterrorism response in Australia and also overseas. Needless to say, casually reading the Sunday paper articles years before about what was to become known as the Bali One bombing didn't have me well prepared for what was rapidly eventuating.

Standing, dripping in the shower, I listened through the avalanche of panicked messages.

'Seven bombs have exploded in Bali, call Stephen back as soon as possible.'

Who the fuck is Stephen? I thought as I hit the 'next' button.

'Sir, can you authorise a forensic team to fly to Bali, it may be better for you to charter a whole flight for AFP personnel, let me know what your decision is please.'

Next: 'Three bombs have exploded in Jakarta, call me back urgently!'

Unlisted number.

Next: 'It's Jo from the Emergency Response Team of Foreign Affairs, I understand you're our new contact, there's an IDETF tomorrow at 9 am, look forward to seeing you then, ta ta.'

IDETF … WTF?

Next: 'It's Roberta from Ministerial, I'm watching CNN, looks like some bombs have exploded in Bali, the minister will want a brief on this first thing in the morning, can you text me the salient points so I can brief him? Thanks.'

NAKED

Next: 'There's some AFP already on the ground in Bali, they were there on holidays, they reckon there'll be a lot of deaths, mostly Aussies … oh by the way, it's Stephen.'

Next: 'David, four flights have left Bali since the bombs exploded, each one could have witnesses, photos, videos and other important evidence. Two flights departed for Australia, one just left for Singapore and the one leaving now is going to Jakarta. There's a Cathay flight leaving for Hong Kong in an hour. Of course we don't want to lose any evidence, can you talk to the various authorities and have the passengers interviewed as they get off in Australia, Singapore and Hong Kong? If they were in Kuta or Jimbaran Bay when the bombs detonated, we'll need to seize their clothing to test for chemical blast residue too.'

Next: 'Hi David, it's John from Intelligence. Sorry I didn't get to talk to you. I expect you're very busy at the moment so I'll just leave a message. I just wanted to let you know that the latest information on JI is that they are planning to be more flexible with their attacks, using smaller bombs concealed in packages, parcels and backpacks. I can give you a full briefing in the Top-Secret vault tomorrow morning but just thought I should let you know in case you think there could be some bombers on the planes that have left Bali – two are destined for Australia.'[8]

I stepped from the shower onto the bath mat and looked straight into the mirror. I had never felt more naked in my

DEFEATING TERROR

life. I held my own gaze for a few seconds as a tidal wave of self-doubt and apprehension crashed its way through my mind and adrenaline flooded my veins. Then, inexplicably, fond images of my many Bali surf trips streamed into my mind's eye: perfect blue water, left-handed barrels, cold Bintangs, cute Balinese children with Hollywood-perfect smiles, wrinkled old women's faces shaded under their conical hats as they beckon me to a beach massage, buying 12 watches I didn't need and getting my nails painted a variety of outrageous colours and designs. Chaotic and charismatic Bali.

The wet phone in my hand suddenly vibrated and rang, smashing through my happy thoughts. I quickly took stock and refocused. Innocent people had once again been murdered in Bali by terrorists. Self-doubt and apprehension were rapidly replaced by anger and determination. I caught my own gaze in the mirror and stared deeply into my eyes. *You've been a federal detective for 15 years*, I thought as the phone continued to ring. *Keep it simple, stick to policing priorities; save and protect lives ... then catch the bastards that did it.*

I took a deep breath, composed myself and answered the phone: 'David speaking.'

'It's Stephen again, I—'

'Stephen, listen very carefully. I want you to give this phone number to the AFP members in Bali. They are no longer on holidays, they're on duty. I want a verbal situation report from the most senior member there every 30 minutes, until I say stop. Do you understand?'

'Yes.'

I had just commenced what would become a 31-hour shift. While I was certainly being singed by a baptism of fire, I wasn't new to running major operations for the AFP. This was another crime investigation, an ugly and complicated crime investigation, but one I vehemently wanted to solve. At the Cairns airport and on the flights to Canberra that night, I read everything I could get my hands on, classified and unclassified, in relation to terrorism in Southeast Asia.

During the night, I dispatched AFP interview teams to every Australian international airport that had incoming flights from Bali, to interview passengers and obtain any photographic and forensic evidence, such as blast residue on clothing. A surprising yet understandable characteristic of people caught up in a major terrorist incident overseas is to immediately get to the airport and fly home. This happened with several people in Kuta and Jimbaran Bay. Immediately after the attacks they simply packed up and boarded the next available flight to Australia. As the flights began to arrive in the early hours of the morning, the interview teams were able to not only secure evidence that would have otherwise been lost, they were able to provide me with first-hand witness accounts in real time.

DEFEATING TERROR

AFP members based in Jakarta travelled during the night and established a Forward Command Post in Bali. The Forward Command Post was established in the Discovery Kartika Plaza Hotel in Kuta where AFP and Indonesian National Police (INP) officers could work side-by-side. This was exactly the same place where the two agencies had worked on the Bali One bombing. History seemed to be repeating itself. Adding irony to irony, when the Kartika Plaza hotel was once again filling up with police officers investigating a Bali bombing, we discovered a film production crew had checked in days before – they were filming a production about Bali One, including events at the Kartika Plaza. In a case of life imitating art, the actors and crew saw firsthand an actual 're-creation' of what had happened three years before.

During the night, the Forward Command Post was a vital source of incoming information. By the time the sun was rising on 2 October 2005, and the media was ablaze with information about the attacks, we had forensic teams travelling to Bali, family liaison officers assigned to support witnesses and victims in Australia, Bali and Singapore, and a team of investigators and intelligence officers flying from Sydney to the Bali Forward Command Post.

I made it, just, to the IDETF in Canberra at 9 am, which I found out stands for Inter-Departmental Emergency Task Force.

Game on.

WHO THE HELL IS JAMAAH ISLAMIYAH?

The IDETF provides a national whole-of-government response to significant incidents overseas. It's chaired by the Department of Foreign Affairs and Trade (DFAT) and each relevant federal agency is represented. By default, I was the AFP representative for this particular emergency. The taxi from Canberra's airport took me into the paved circular drive at the front of the RG Casey DFAT Building on John McEwen Crescent, past the sad-looking Australian flag resting at half-mast.

After dropping off my overnight bag at security, I joined the growing queue of suits and skirts filing through the security screening point into the highly polished cavernous foyer. A crammed lift ride later, I spilt out with others into an anteroom where everyone's phone was locked in individual phone lockers.

DEFEATING TERROR

Classified meetings prohibited the possession of communication devices. Polite banter ensued between some of the suits and skirts, who clearly knew each other and had obviously attended IDETFs before. As we waited for the medieval-scale wooden doors to be opened, I looked around the congregation of 40 or so senior executives; I held a confident posture, but shrank two sizes inside my suit.

Finally, the doors yawned and we flowed into the boardroom. In the centre were 20 high-backed leather chairs pushed tightly into place against a long leather-topped mahogany table. Surrounding the table concentrically were three rows of seating, for the less important, that were being quickly occupied. By comparison the AFP is a relatively small Commonwealth agency, so I took my place at one of those.

Amongst the hubbub, I heard someone at the centre table comment, 'The AFP aren't here?'

Heads swivelled and eyes darted around the room. Like a guilty schoolchild, I raised my hand.

'That would be me,' I confessed, glancing at my watch, as if it could give me some credibility for not knowing where to sit. Rather awkwardly I ushered myself to the vacant place at the headmaster's table.

What was discussed at that meeting remains classified. However, I can reassure those who have never attended an IDETF that these meetings, and the people who attend them,

WHO THE HELL IS JAMAAH ISLAMIYAH?

are completely committed to interdepartmental cooperation and providing vital assistance to Australians overseas. If you are in trouble overseas, know that these people will be doing everything they can to assist you.

Perhaps naively, I thought I wouldn't have much to contribute to the high-powered intragovernmental meeting. However, not long after the meeting commenced, I quickly learned that as a result of the AFP 'boots on the ground' in Bali and my continuous updates throughout the night, I was better placed than most at the table in respect to the current situation in Bali. It was critical that everyone in the room had the most accurate and up-to-date information. Without being the bombastic newcomer, I provided a verbal briefing on what had actually occurred the previous night, dispelling some of the inevitable misinformation that is generated in the early stages of a major crisis. I was also able to give a contemporaneous situation report based on information I had received just prior to turning my phone off and locking it away, just minutes before the meeting commenced. By the end of the IDETF I'd grown back into my suit – but it wasn't tight.

Through the IDETF, a crisis hotline was established and a special Qantas flight and two RAAF C-130 Hercules aircraft with specialist medical teams were dispatched to Bali to bring victims to Darwin Hospital. Others, including Terry and Jessica Fitzgerald, were medevaced to Singapore, where they were met by Terry Fitzgerald's parents, Trevor and Win. Jessica had regained consciousness after suffering burns and shrapnel wounds, whereas Terry remained unconscious and critically ill. At that stage, neither had been advised of Brendan's death.

Following the IDETF I responded to the avalanche of new phone messages that had accumulated during the meeting as I taxied to the AFP headquarters on the corner of Northbourne Avenue and Bunda Street in Canberra's CBD. Almost immediately I attended another phone-free boardroom meeting, this time chaired by the AFP commissioner. During the meeting I was nominated as the senior investigating officer (SIO) and operational commander for AFP Operation Affinity, the investigative response to the second Bali attack.

After that, I made my way to the Commander of Counterterrorism office and shut the door. I plonked myself into the office chair, simultaneously hit the power button on the computer and my mobile phone and absorbed the solace of the room and the gentle whir of the computer's hard drive as it gained speed. Inevitably, this peaceful moment was shattered by a cascade of new message alerts bleating for attention.

By 1 pm that day, less than 24 hours after the explosions, we had managed to land a team of 32 officers at the Bali Forward Command Post from a variety of disciplines including forensics, bomb data, disaster victim identification, investigators, intelligence and family liaison officers. The Bali

WHO THE HELL IS JAMAAH ISLAMIYAH?

Forward Command Post was led by a detective superintendent who reported directly to me. Additionally, in Canberra there was a 24-hour Incident Coordination Centre (ICC) established that received and processed information from all sources, including regional AFP counterterrorism teams, airport interview teams, overseas liaison officers and members of the public. The superintendent in charge of the ICC also reported directly to me. I, in turn, reported directly to AFP senior management.

Amidst the rapid flow of information I was receiving through email and phone messages, I needed to gain an understanding as to why Bali had been bombed again. I already knew the Bali One bombing was carried out by JI and that they were a radical Islamic group. Years before, when I read about that attack in newspapers, it was easy, perhaps too easy, to reconcile that it was a one-off group of religious fanatics.

In the past, I had travelled to Indonesia several times, predominantly to Bali and Lombok on surfing holidays. I had made friends with Hindu and Muslim Indonesians; their religion to me was irrelevant. I liked them and I liked their culture. I had even enrolled in a Bahasa Indonesia course so I could better learn and understand their language and culture. In my mind, these were good people and it was hard to comprehend the level of hatred motivating some of them to the point of indiscriminate mass murder.

I well understood that within any society there can be a few mentally defective murderers, but from what I'd read in Cairns the night before and on the flights to Canberra, it appeared JI wasn't just a few lunatics. JI was a well-organised, well-funded religious movement that glorified suicide and had on several occasions successfully motivated some of its members to murderous martyrdom in the name of Islam.

In the past, I'd simplistically thought a parallel could be drawn between Islamic groups such as JI and the Irish terror group the IRA, which had wrought bombing havoc in the UK for decades. However, from what I had read, there appeared to be some glaring fundamental differences. The IRA were definitely fanatics, they definitely killed people and they definitely bombed buildings. But they didn't glorify religious suicide. Additionally, the IRA sometimes gave forewarning of their bombs, so people could be evacuated before the device was exploded. Strategically, this was done to achieve the terror outcome without killing innocent members of the public, which could lead to more people being motivated against the IRA. JI had never given a forewarning – they just wanted to kill. JI somehow motivated people to not only kill themselves but also innocent people, of any religion, including their own. To me it was unfathomable.

By 2 pm on that first day, the established facts in Bali were that about 20 people had been murdered and more than 100

WHO THE HELL IS JAMAAH ISLAMIYAH?

people injured the night before. A tactical investigation was needed to pursue every line of enquiry emanating from the crime scenes. This was predominantly the responsibility of the INP and AFP at the Bali Forward Command Post. They were sifting through all the tactical information from the crime scenes and had been regularly briefing me on developments and completing lines of enquiry I sent them.

In addition to the tactical investigation in Bali, an important component of my role at the time was a strategic one: to identify those who had funded and organised the attack, assist the Indonesians to arrest those responsible and, critically, to prevent any potential future attack.

I had full confidence in the personnel at the Forward Command Post, and I'd led high-profile investigations before. While it wasn't a walk in the park for me by any means, as it was a highly complex international case, I was, relatively speaking, comfortable with the tactical aspect of the investigation. What I wasn't comfortable with was my lack of insight into JI – the organisation that everyone kept telling me was most likely behind this latest attack.

Most AFP agents who were now working for me in counterterrorism had experience with JI and the first Bali investigation. I did not. They knew who the offenders were, they knew who had been apprehended and who was still on the run. They also knew the history that led up to the first

31

bombing and, importantly, how it was carried out. I knew very little about these things. If I was to lead this investigation effectively and have a chance at mitigating the potential for a future attack, I needed to better understand the events leading up to today.

Ever since leaving Cairns, I'd been playing a desperate game of knowledge catch-up. Finally, now most of the investigative infrastructure in Indonesia and Australia was in place, I needed to take some time to better understand JI.

Deep within the bowels of AFP headquarters was a top secret-rated information vault that held documents of the highest classification for the organisation.[9] About the size of a two-bedroom unit, the white steel–lined gargantuan safe housed thousands of documents and some workstations for the few staff who worked diligently inside, bereft of daylight, to protect and, where appropriate, to share that information. I contacted the vault staff and requested the latest highly classified intelligence package on JI.

About 3.30 pm, one of the vault staff knocked gently and entered the office. He placed a bright-red satchel on my desk and un-padlocked the zip. I signed a receipt and retrieved about a ream's worth of typed information.[10] The vault employee then took a seat outside the office and settled in as though he was getting ready to watch a movie. *Surely you're not going to sit there while I read all this*, I thought.

WHO THE HELL IS JAMAAH ISLAMIYAH?

'I can ring you when I've finished, if you like,' I offered.

'No, it's fine, I'm the custodian and have to stay with the documents until they're back in the vault.'

'It might be a while mate, I'm a slow reader.'

'That's fine,' he said courteously.

This is what I learned …

WIRING THE ISLAMIC KILL-SWITCH

Abdullah Achmad bin Sungkar (Sungkar)[11] and Abu Bakar Bashir (Bashir)[12] were Indonesians of Yemeni descent who met in 1963. Both men shunned democracy and had a shared vision that the Indonesian government would enforce Sharia law and create an Islamic-only state. In 1967, they rented a small cottage in Solo (also referred to as Surakarta) in Central Java and used a radio transmitter to broadcast their forceful free-to-air firebrand preaching to anyone who would listen. A combination of their risky anti-government messages, provocative preaching and credible Middle Eastern ethnicity allowed them to gain a foothold in the minds of many around Solo.

Building on their popularity, the pair founded the Al-Mukmin *pesantren* (a term for an Islamic boarding school) in

WIRING THE ISLAMIC KILL-SWITCH

Ngruki in the eastern suburbs of Solo in 1973.[13] There, board and lodging was provided for the male-only students. Typical of many *pesantren*, the children were separated from their parents and encouraged to form a close bond with the teachers and their teachings. In normal circumstances this can be a beneficial educative environment. However, not when the teachers are of the ilk of Sungkar and Bashir, who now had unfettered 24-hour access to instil hatred, racism and intolerance into vulnerable minds.

A typical day for the students commenced at 3 am and concluded around 10 pm. During that time the boys were subjected to arduous hours of Koranic study, Arabic language training, Islamic law, Islamic code of conduct and radical speeches from an array of already radicalised teachers.

If the long hours, mental fatigue and myopic, racist view of the world weren't enough to incite religious intolerance in the students during class time, there were playtime reminders as well. A reporter who visited Al-Mukmin wrote:

> Where a school elsewhere might have little signs near the
> playground reminding students that a healthy body is a
> healthy mind, Al-Mukmin students head off for a bout
> of football or martial arts reminded by painted signs that
> say, 'Death in the Way of Allah Is Our Biggest Aspiration'.
> Another sign, illustrated with a tank firing its gun asks,

DEFEATING TERROR

'Jihad? Why Not?' As teams play a vigorous game of volleyball on the dusty outside court they are instructed that there is, 'No Prestige Without Jihad.' [14]

Adding weight to their already significant psychological leverage over the children, the school deliberately isolated the students from the outside world. It banned television, radio and even singing. The students lived according to Sharia law where students were taught, amongst other things, that:

- criticising or denying any part of the Koran or that Mohammed is a prophet is punishable by death
- a Muslim who becomes a non-Muslim should be put to death
- a man can have up to four wives; a woman can only have one husband
- a man may legally beat his wife for insubordination
- a woman's court testimony is only allowed in property cases and her testimony is worth half that of a man
- Muslims should lie to non-Muslims to advance Islam
- homosexuality is punishable by death
- martyrdom (suicide) in a violent Jihad is to be idolised and aspired to.[15]

WIRING THE ISLAMIC KILL-SWITCH

All this was enforced in a highly disciplined environment where physical assaults for non-compliance were not infrequent.[16] It was a toxic environment of intolerance and aggression towards anyone not living according to the strict Sharia code. This was no ordinary Islamic education facility. The children believed they were part of a holy war between Islam and every other religion, where democracy, equality and freedom of speech were despised and suicide in the name of Islam was the ultimate gift.

After years in such an environment, their otherwise innocent free-thinking minds were understandably manipulated, moulded and indelibly marked; some to the point of being psychologically wired with an Islamic 'kill-switch'. It could be self-activated in revenge for perceived attacks on Islam or if facing adverse circumstances in life, motivated by the belief of afterlife rewards for martyrs and their families. The Islamic kill-switch could also be activated externally by an astute recruiter, in person or, as the future would reveal, to great effect via the internet.

Under the guise of education, Bashir and Sungkar were establishing their very own Islamic Hitler Youth program. It would have been bad enough if there was only one such school. Alas, the hate virus found traction in the minds of many in Central Java and the infection spread, increasing the number of radical *pesantren* to more than 20 institutions in the following years.

In 1976, Sungkar, Bashir and Hispran, the deputy commander of radical Islamic group Komando Jihad, met in Solo and decided to form Jamaah Islamiyah, an Islamic community group that would live and fight strictly according to their interpretation of the Koran – and whose enemies would be anyone that didn't, including the Indonesian government.

In November 1978, Sungkar and Bashir were arrested for subversion, based on Hispran's confessions of the joint plan to form Jamaah Islamiyah. It was also alleged that Sungkar was the military commander of Darul Islam in Central Java – a fanatical Islamic group the Indonesian government had been fighting for decades.

The arrests and the trial catapulted both Sungkar and Bashir into the spotlight, attracting the admiration and support of radically inclined Muslims. The number of parents who sent their teenage boys to the Al-Mukmin boarding school and those modelled off it increased, as did the number of toxic brainwashed alumni they produced. In 1982 both men were found guilty of subversion and were sentenced to 9 years' jail, but were later released on appeal, for time served.

Their time in jail and in the media spotlight simply added credibility to their cause when they returned to Solo in 1982. Both men would have been immensely satisfied that Al-Mukmin and its replicas were flourishing and their Islamic Hitler Youth program had grown during their four-

WIRING THE ISLAMIC KILL-SWITCH

year absence. The quantity of students was rapidly expanding as was the quality of the graduates: many had a violent Jihadic propensity. Indicative of the Al-Mukmin alumni at that time were three brothers, Mukhlas, Amrozi and Imron, whose Islamic kill-switches will lead two of them to war and all three of them to mass murder in Bali.[17] One will be remorseful and remain for the rest of his life behind bars; the other two will remain defiant until executed.

Sungkar and Bashir were now high-profile figures and knew they were of ongoing interest to the Indonesian government. To continue their insidious work without intervention, they needed to learn from the past and adapt. Since the 1950s Darul Islam had openly fought the government, which resulted in that organisation eventually being disbanded by government military action – so overt violence needed to be minimised. Both men had just spent four years in jail for publicly espousing Islamic law and denouncing democracy and the government. To avoid being incarcerated again, a new discreet measure of communication and influence was needed. In answer to this, they formed an Islamic study group called an 'usroh'.

Members of the usroh were sworn to secrecy and to always deny its existence. Externally the close-knit group appeared to be an innocent religious study group holding regular meetings. However, the usroh model had been taken from the Middle East, where groups could form and share radical ideas under the guise of religious study. Using that cover, the *usroh*'s purpose was to spread Jamaah Islamiyah's message and build networks of like-minded radicals throughout Indonesia that could act discreetly and independently towards creating an Islamic state. Once an Islamic state had been established in Indonesia, the program was to expand into other countries; the ultimate goal was worldwide Islamic domination.

The Ngruki *usroh*'s model rapidly spread throughout Java, effectively forming a human internet across the country. This was greatly enhanced by the continual churning out of intolerant radicalised students from the increasing number of *pesantren*. Unlike Darul Islam, which predominantly recruited its members from uneducated, poor rural areas, JI was able to use the *usroh* model to expand their fundamentalist study groups into mosques on university campuses.

So, joining the ranks of disaffected poor and radicalised youths from the *pesantren* were intellectuals and academics; this exponentially expanded the organisation's sphere of influence in the community. However, under Indonesian president Suharto's reign, there was little tolerance for intolerance. The Suharto government reinforced Indonesia's founding system of democracy (*Pancasila*) and it cracked down on violent Islamic groups who were opposed to living in a democratic society.

In 1983, police arrested 40 *usroh* members in quick succession, sending shock waves through the groups. One of those arrested confessed that Sungkar and Bashir had circulated documents urging Muslims to go to war against anyone who resisted Islamic law and to ignore national laws and the courts if it conflicted in any way with the Koran.

More arrests followed but, for reasons unknown, these didn't include Sungkar and Bashir. However, in February 1985, the Supreme Court summonsed them to a hearing. The pair knew it was only a matter of time until they were arrested once again.[18] So they and seven Ngruki *usroh* members fled to Malaysia, leaving others to face a renewed government crackdown.

A FERTILE FIELD

At that time, Malaysia had a virtual open door policy for Islamic extremists, so Sungkar and Bashir had no difficulty crossing the Malacca Strait by boat and settling in a rented villa in Jempol, about 140 kilometres south-east of Kuala Lumpur.[19] The pair convinced themselves, and anyone else who would listen, that they had made a tactical withdrawal, rather than scampering in the face of adversity. Via the *usroh* network they sent word back to other JI members, encouraging them to leave Indonesia and to continue JI's objectives from Malaysia.

Unknown to either of them at the time was the fact that fate was dealing them a future winning hand in the form of a 25-year-old Adelaide University student – his name was Azhari bin Husin (Azhari).[20]

While Sungkar and Bashir were establishing a Malaysian *usroh* as a new chapter in the ever-sprawling network, Azhari had just completed his fourth year in the faculty of engineering at the University of Adelaide and was preparing to return to

A FERTILE FIELD

his native Malaysia. Since arriving in Australia to study four years previously, he'd totally embraced Australian culture, particularly the social and drinking side. Engineering students are legendary in most universities for their heavy drinking and partying. Azhari held his own and had a well-earned reputation as one of the engineering faculty's party-animal elite. Despite being naturally shy, he had a wickedly quick sense of humour and he participated in a variety of sports, excelling at soccer. His humour and have-a-go attitude had ingratiated him with his Australian friends, one of whom described him as 'a guy who could always make people laugh'.[21]

While Azhari was in Adelaide, headlines regularly revolved around the activities of the Ayatollah Khomeini, who had returned from exile and subsequently been declared the supreme religious leader of the Islamic Republic of Iran after toppling the remnants of its government. Khomeini had for years been spitting his disgust at everything non-Islamic, and now he was in a position to spread his Islamofascism further.[22]

While living in exile, Khomeini used propaganda videos to promote his cause. Now using the Iranian state media that he controlled, he had the worldwide platform he'd been seeking. Via this medium, Khomeini encouraged Muslims to fight a holy war against Jews, the West and, of course, democracy:

Don't listen to those who speak of democracy. They all are against Islam. They want to take the nation away from its mission. We will break all the poison pens of those who speak of nationalism, democracy, and such things.[23]

Despite Khomeini's violent Islamic revolution being led by Shiite Muslims it also had an inspirational effect across the Indonesian archipelago where the majority of Muslims were Sunni.[24] Khomeini's oratory toxins infected the minds of many Muslims around the world, but apparently not Azhari. As a moderate Muslim living in Australia, Azhari seemed immune to such calls-to-arms. He couldn't be radicalised. Yet.

While in Australia, Azhari had lived a fun-filled and carefree campus life. Unfortunately, he was returning to Malaysia with a secret he hadn't shared with anyone, least of all his parents, who had funded his study. For the past four years, he'd been failing most of his subjects. This was more a product of his social activities than his intelligence. Azhari had a mind like a steel trap, particularly when it came to mathematics, technology and electronics. However, his passion for partying had a significant impact on his academic results – a card he had, until now, played very close to his chest.

Like other university students in a similar predicament, it most likely started with a white lie told to his parents to cover his failure of a subject in the very first semester. Perhaps

A FERTILE FIELD

wrongly, he assumed that he could continue an active social life and pick up the additional workload of the failed subject during the following semester. However, the additional workload snowballed, as no doubt did the lies surrounding his progress at university. Now it was all coming to an end.

In Malaysia, his proud parents were looking forward to seeing their son and for him to commence work as an engineer. After a four-year folly, it was time for Azhari to face the music: he had no choice but to make a full confession to his father and to make amends for his shortcomings. This was a defining moment in Azhari's life. It appears at that juncture he made a commitment to completely turn his life around and devote his time to continuous learning and improvement. These qualities would have seen him upwardly mobile in any organisation. He didn't know it then – nobody knew it then – but his future organisation of choice would be JI.

After his arrival in Kuala Lumpur, he faced the wrath of his father and the tears of his mother. However, true to his word, he enrolled in an undergraduate degree in Malaysia. His university life there was the polar opposite of what it had been in Australia, as was his social life. Azhari, it appears, became withdrawn. He stopped drinking alcohol, didn't attend parties and he didn't re-establish relationships with many of his Malaysian friends – in fact he rarely had time for anything except satisfying his drive to achieve. As a result, his academic results were outstanding and his social life abysmal, with one exception: her name was Wan Nur Aini Jusoh (Nur Aini).

Nur Aini was also studying at the university. Azhari and Nur Aini completed their undergraduate degrees and were married in Johor, Malaysia in November 1985. By the end of that year Azhari had been accepted by Reading University in the UK to complete a master's degree in statistical modelling. The newly married couple left for the UK to commence a new and exciting time together.

Britain's cold would have initially been a shock for the two Malaysians as they settled in to their modest one-bedroom flat. Considering he was newly married, had excelled at university and was destined for a master's degree in the UK, it's reasonable to assume that at this stage, Azhari had a significant weight lifted off his shoulders and some of his lightheartedness and sociability returned. He reacquainted himself with alcohol and became a light social drinker, but he certainly wasn't going to deviate from his goals, as he had in Australia.

It wasn't long before Azhari's academic supervisor noticed the quality of his research and recommended him to the faculty board for PhD candidature. When the board found in favour of this recommendation, Azhari and Nur Aini must've been ecstatic. The pair would have chatted excitedly about what this would mean for their future. At the time, the Southeast Asian economy was booming, and real estate with it. Azhari's PhD was

A FERTILE FIELD

in statistical modelling, a field highly applicable to real estate. The timing was perfect. When his research was completed, they would be destined for both wealth and prestige.

Around this time, Nur Aini found out she was pregnant. It's hard to imagine a happier time in Nur Aini's and Azhari's lives. Azhari, particularly, would have been truly and deeply happy for the first time in many years. From Nur Aini's perspective, not only was she going to be a mother, but the man she married had also transformed from being socially isolated and withdrawn into a goldmine of charm and wit.

For the pair of them, the next few weeks would have been bliss. However, this changed dramatically when Nur Aini discovered she was no longer pregnant. This understandably would have been gut-wrenching for the couple. Nur Aini has a deeply caring nature and the event no doubt weighed heavily on her. Equally, though, she's a strong-minded woman and no doubt she managed to right herself. Not so for Azhari. His darkened mood and withdrawn self returned. Compounding this over the following months was the fact that Nur Aini now seemed unable to fall pregnant again.

It was either convenient timing, a planned strategy to lift their moods, or simply that they missed the warmth of both Malaysia and their immediate families, that the pair returned to their homeland for the Eid al-Fitr celebrations – the most festive period on the Islamic calendar.[25] They spent four weeks at Nur Aini's parents' house at Taman Desa Keramat, an outer suburb of Kuala Lumpur.

At some stage during that stay, Azhari became aware of a revolutionary Muslim cleric from Indonesia who was holding public presentations. At that time, Taman Desa Keramat was a picturesque but predominantly poor rural area with high unemployment and a struggling underclass. Azhari came from a very different background: his parents were educated and financially comfortable. So, it's likely he assumed the cleric's speech would have been simply a religious meeting to give the poor community hope about their future; hardly relevant to his own circumstances. Regardless, for one reason or another, Azhari attended and for the first time saw and heard Sungkar.

Despite being a poor area, Taman Desa Keramat was surrounded by fertile farming land. When Sungkar delivered his public sermon, it wasn't the fertile land he was wanting to nurture — it was the fertile minds of the disheartened. Sungkar, a charismatic and passionate performer, knew his audiences, often tapping into community frustration. He would have asked some of his typical rhetorical questions of the crowd, such as, 'Is life hard?', 'Are you looking for happiness?', 'Do you feel lost?', and 'Why is life so hard? Have you ever asked yourself why this is so?'

Sungkar's answer to these questions was always simple: America, Britain, their allies and the Jews were manipulating

A FERTILE FIELD

the world so they got rich and Muslims had to struggle. Islam was the only way that they could fulfil their lives and defend themselves against democracy and the immoral ways of the West. The answer was Sharia law – the law of Islam.

Explaining his Indonesian accent and promoting his ethnicity, Sungkar often played up his Yemeni background and the fact that national borders shouldn't be recognised as these are defined by governments, not the Koran. According to Sungkar, there was only Muslim land, and land that should be Muslim land. Like many other radicals, the ultimate goal for Sungkar and Bashir was for the entire world to be Islamic and to live under Sharia law.

The pair were convinced there was a holy war taking place, and they did their best to draw others into their perceived fight. The less-educated were easy fodder for the educated Muslim clerics, who were naturally afforded respect in such circles. From an apparent platform of religious authority, Sungkar often spruiked that in the Koran, on 480 occasions, Allah instructs Muslims to wage Jihad against non-believers.[26] That Muslims are at war, therefore they must act as they are at war. As a respected Muslim cleric, by the end of the night Sungkar had no doubt successfully planted the seeds of blame and hatred in some vulnerable desperate minds.

Despite coming from an entirely different background to most in the audience that night, some of Sungkar's sentiments struck a chord with Azhari. At that juncture, life for him was hard. They had had a miscarriage and now, it appeared that Nur Aini would be unable to give him a son. Azhari had come from a moderate and progressive Muslim background, as had Nur Aini, but Sungkar's sermon must have stirred something deep inside him.

Either that night or some time shortly thereafter, Azhari met with Sungkar for the first time. It would have been immediately apparent to Sungkar, by Azhari's enunciation and vocabulary, that he was an educated man. Azhari's quality clothes also would have differentiated him from the majority that attended public sermons. When Azhari explained his struggles, including their loss in the UK, how it seemed Nur Aini could no longer fall pregnant, his academic failure and a past of drinking, gambling, partying and promiscuity in Australia, Sungkar would have treaded his well-worn path of blaming everything on Azhari for not living strictly according to the Koran. Consequently, Azhari was now doing penance for his indiscretions and nothing would change until he made a wholesale life-change and committed to living strictly according to Sharia law.

These statements should have been irrational to a man with a scientific education. But Azhari *was* vulnerable. He *was* lost. Sungkar offered a reason why things had gone wrong for Nur Aini and himself. At that point in Azhari's life, Sungkar's

A FERTILE FIELD

spiritual advice and reassuring remedy were the warm glove for the cold hand of Azhari's life. It fitted and it was comfortable. For Azhari, Sungkar offered a pathway out of his mire. As for Sungkar, he had expertly planted a seed in a very fertile field.

RIPE FRUIT

Azhari and Nur Aini returned to Reading and their lives resumed their regular routine. Now, though, Azhari was dividing his academic intellect between his doctoral research at university and studying the Koran.

Despite Azhari's newfound direction, Sungkar's fiery urging to live by and interpret the Koran strictly remained at odds with Azhari's upbringing. He had come from a progressive Muslim community that didn't interpret the Koran literally for guidance of their day-to-day lives. The result was a peaceful Muslim community that adapted to a modern Islamic way of life. No doubt Azhari respected the fact that Nur Aini had attained a university degree, which under Sharia law would have been prohibited – her education would have been limited solely to the Koran. Nur Aini was an educated, intelligent and independent woman. Azhari was eagerly pursuing his academic passion and, together, they were enjoying a free and tranquil life. So, during this period it's likely Azhari psychologically

RIPE FRUIT

wrestled with the comfortable glove and the peaceful reality of his life in London.

Apart from Azhari starting to study the Koran more closely, it's not clear how much influence Sungkar's words had on Azhari's psyche. However, in the months that followed, when Nur Aini advised him that she was once again pregnant it must have seemed proof positive that living closer to the Koran was mitigating his penance. While Nur Aini falling pregnant may have seemed a validation for some of what Sungkar had told him, it's likely, considering Azhari's progressive Muslim upbringing, that he would have been conflicted by other parts, such as Sungkar's literal Koranic interpretations arguing against gender equality and democracy. At this juncture, it appears Azhari was still resistant to radicalisation.

While Azhari was working towards completing his third and final year of research, Mukhlas (aka Ali Ghufron), an Indonesian Ngruki graduate and protege of Bashir, was coming to the end of his three-year Jihadic sabbatical in Afghanistan. During that time, Mukhlas had been based predominantly in Kandahar, where he was taught a wide variety of combat skills. He had applied these skills on many occasions in skirmishes with Soviet troops. Mukhlas had a natural leadership style that inspired others.

The proudest moment in his three-year combat apprenticeship was in April 1987. According to Mukhlas's

53

account, he was part of a large group of *mujahedin* who were returning to Kandahar on trucks after launching a surprise attack on a Soviet camp. With the snow melting early that year, it had allowed them to launch the spring offensive earlier than usual, successfully catching the Soviet camp underprepared.[27] Shortly after getting off the truck, Mukhlas saw the unmistakably lanky figure of Osama bin Laden.

Sometime later, Mukhlas was introduced to bin Laden. They then had a short conversation, the content of which is unknown. Bin Laden then moved on to meet other *mujahedin*. However, according to Mukhlas, the moment didn't move on in his mind: it stayed with him as his life's proudest moment. If there was ever a chance of Mukhlas becoming a peaceful Muslim, that chance had now passed; his Islamic kill-switch was locked on.

Travelling with bin Laden at the time was another Indonesian, a lot higher up in the world terrorist pecking order than Mukhlas. His name was Hambali, and he was a trusted associate of bin Laden who spoke fluent Arabic.[28] With the intention of creating an active network in Southeast Asia parallel to his newly formed Al-Qaeda, bin Laden had nominated Hambali as his representative in that area. By design Hambali became chief of operations for JI. He was the golden product of Islamic teaching at a *pesantren* in West Java, which had psychologically stained him for life. As a *pesantren* graduate

RIPE FRUIT

and past student of both Bashir and Sungkar, he was the logical choice. It's likely that about the time bin Laden met Mukhlas, or shortly thereafter, Hambali put Mukhlas, a graduate of the same *pesantren*, forward to bin Laden to take over the Luqmanul Hakiem Islamic School (LHIS) in Johor, Malaysia.

The LHIS was a fledgling version of the Al-Mukmin *pesantren* in Ngruki and was desperately in need of funding. Bin Laden, who had that funding and more, would have been acutely aware of the Indonesian government's stance against radicalising *pesantren* in Indonesia at the time, and the lackadaisical approach by the Malaysian government towards terrorist institutions. With the assurance of spiritual guidance being provided by Bashir and Sungkar, the proposition found favour with bin Laden.

Mukhlas returned from Afghanistan and, on 1 July 1990, he was married in Johor, Malaysia.[29] As instructed by Hambali and Bashir, Mukhlas immediately started working with others, including his younger brother Amrozi, to expand the LHIS.[30]

The school was deliberately promoted as a peaceful Islamic boarding school. However, as was the case in the JI-funded schools in Indonesia, behind closed doors the focus was anything but peace-focused. Under Mukhlas the school became a micro Islamic State, filled with radical rhetoric where racism, hatred and intolerance were preached from dawn till after dusk. The desperate need for each male student to help deliver a worldwide Islamic caliphate ruled by Sharia law was reinforced, reinforced and reinforced again. Christians, Jews and the West were incessantly blamed for the poor state of Muslim countries and for waging a perceived holy war against Islam.

It was almost the twenty-first century and the status of women had been advanced in many Muslim countries, but not at this school. The teaching stuck to strictly to the Koran, using it to reinforce that women were inferior to men, unclean when menstruating and should be beaten for disobedience. This is not a criticism of the Koran, as many ancient religious and cultural texts (including the Bible) have equally abhorrent passages. What is shocking is that these concepts were being taught to modern-day children. The evil was not in the text – but how it was taught. Mukhlas and his younger brother, Amrozi, had been successfully radicalised at the Al-Mukmin *pesantren* in Ngruki and both relished the opportunity to spread radical Islam in another country – to the next generation of Islamic Hitler Youth.

On 7 July 1990, a week after Mukhlas's marriage, Azhari was awarded a PhD from Reading University and returned almost immediately to Taman Desa Keramat, Malaysia to live with Nur Aini and her parents. Three months later their first child, Aisyah, a healthy daughter, was born.[31] Azhari taught statistics for a time at University of Technology Malaysia

RIPE FRUIT

(UTM), Johor, and over the next few years he focused his significant mathematical ability on property management and real estate valuation theory. With the Indonesian economy booming, Azhari saw the opportunity to secure a good income working in the real estate industry in Jakarta. In 1996 he was contracted as a director for a property consultancy. So he, Nur Aini and baby Aisyah moved to Indonesia.

While in Jakarta, Nur Aini started regularly feeling fatigued. However, without a definitive medical diagnosis, life continued. Despite this ailment, it was an enjoyable time for Azhari's family. Aisyah brought another dimension to Azhari's loving marriage with Nur Aini and his job was lucrative. According to his colleagues, Azhari had a nervous laugh and displayed an introverted demeanour, keeping largely to himself and avoiding social engagements: exactly the opposite of what he had been in Adelaide.[32]

There is no indication that Azhari had walked the plank any further towards radicalisation during his time in Indonesia. However, catching the bus past the Australian embassy each day on his way to work could not have gone unnoticed by Azhari, the flag perhaps reminding him of his past failure. At this time, he was a devoted family man and property consultant. But in just a few short years he would return to that very place as a highly trained, ruthless Islamic radical, with a 1-tonne bomb aimed at the mass murder of Australians.

DEFEATING TERROR

In 1997, about 12 months after arriving in Jakarta, there was a sharp economic downturn in the Asian economies, including Indonesia. The ramifications were widespread and Azhari had to leave his high-paying job. Following this, he did some guest lecturing for six months at Gadjah Mada University, Yogyakarta, in the faculty of economics, but it wasn't enough to sustain their lifestyle.

Azhari had no choice but to return to Malaysia where he returned to UTM to lecture. Despite taking a pay cut, working for the faculty of engineering and geo-information science still provided a comfortable salary. This enabled the family to move into a modest three-bedroom house in Taman Teratai, just 5 kilometres from the UTM campus.

While the two men had never met, Azhari's new home was only a short scooter ride from Mukhlas's LHIS *pesantren*, now a thriving terrorist educational facility for children. At some stage subsequent to starting at UTM, Azhari visited the LHIS and met with Sungkar and Bashir. It's possible that Mukhlas was also present. It's also likely it was at that meeting that Azhari was first given a compendium of radicalising Islamic material. These types of books and articles, often circulated by institutions such as this, are written by hardline extremists with the sole purpose of motivating Muslims to violence. Often they include Arabic script from the Koran, which the reader does not understand, but the interpretation in their native language is highly inflammatory.

58

RIPE FRUIT

It's not known why Azhari went to the LHIS for that meeting. He may have simply wanted to meet Sungkar again, or perhaps he was invited by fellow UTM lecturer Wan Min bin Wan Mat, who had been involved with JI since its inception. Or it could be speculated that life events such as losing his high-paying job in Jakarta, or having a daughter instead of a son, or Nur Aini's mysterious illness, or even the daily sighting of the Australian flag from his bus seat in Jakarta, or a combination of all this, culminated in him feeling uneasy and in need of spiritual guidance. Regardless of his reasoning, meeting Sungkar and Bashir and having access to radicalising material definitely stirred something ugly inside Azhari.

Both clerics were charismatic and projected assuredness that Azhari no doubt found comfort in. Surreptitiously, the men psychologically lassoed Azhari with the radical rhetoric and tethered him firmly to the JI path. They slowly drew him in as he attended more meetings at the LHIS. Gradually, the radical Koranic interpretations that would have previously been unpalatable would have seemed less extreme and more interesting to Azhari's inquiring mind. By design these violently biased interpretations are meant to 'rationally' fill gaps in the reader's knowledge about the Koran and open windows to a new way of thinking about Islam. But the windows this radicalising material opened for Azhari didn't provide a peaceful vista of the world. The only solutions it offered were glorifying death and the eradication of anyone who didn't convert to the same form of Islam – including other Muslims.

Nur Aini would later state,

> His thought about Islam was getting stronger when he was actively involved in religious meetings in Luqmanul Hakiem Islamic boarding school ... After being active in numerous religious meetings, he leaned more to religion, slowly he reduced his activities as a lecturer and researcher.[33]

Some weeks after the first meeting at LHIS, Nur Aini discovered that she was pregnant once again. During the pregnancy, Azhari increasingly spent more time studying the Koran and visiting the LHIS. It's possible his rationale for investing more faith in religion at this point was to reduce the possibility of another miscarriage, or perhaps to increase the chances of having a son. When Nur Aini gave birth to their son, Zaid Abil, it would have seemed like a validation for Azhari: that absorbing and believing a more radical perspective of Islam had paid dividends. It was confirmation of what Sungkar and Bashir were preaching.

The following year, Nur Aini started lecturing at UTM and life couldn't be better. The additional income allowed them to have a live-in nanny and housekeeper and to nicely

RIPE FRUIT

furnish their home. They were also able to take short trips to Singapore for weekends away shopping, dining and sightseeing. Their family life was comfortable and to Azhari it would have seemed as though he had served his penance. However, this idyllic period came to a horrific end one day when Nur Aini informed Azhari that her illness had been diagnosed as thyroid cancer. Azhari was no doubt shell-shocked when he was told that an operation was urgently needed and the best-case outcome was that Nur Aini would permanently lose her voice. At that crisis point, Azhari would have felt as though his atonement was far from complete and that future suffering was likely. This manifested after surgery when Nur Aini's voice deteriorated to an almost inaudible husky croak, which led to losing her lecturing job and the income they were reliant on.

Consumed by a cocktail of anger, depression and frustration, Azhari may have felt like Allah was torturing him, teaching him and testing him. Faced with the future possibility of losing his wife and becoming a single father of two children, reparations had to be made. Azhari needed to do more than just research his religion – he needed to act. He had read and now believed that all his sins would be expunged if he were to die fighting a Jihad. Later, at a secret ceremony Azhari swore the JI oath of allegiance in Arabic: 'I offer my allegiance to you, to listen to and obey the orders of God and His message to the best of my ability.'[34] During the induction, like other JI members had in the past, Azhari would have been lectured on the importance of keeping the name 'Jamaah Islamiyah' secret and never to admit such an organisation existed. In addition to being radicalised, Azhari was now completely and officially indoctrinated in the organisation.

Sungkar and Bashir were pleased – the fruit was finally ripe.

MILF

Jamaah Islamiyah's *usroh* network, which was still being successfully sold as a network of innocent prayer groups, continued to peddle their poison, infecting numerous university mosques in Indonesia and Malaysia. This resulted in the conversion and recruitment of several university students. While the mainstays of JI's ranks were still drawn from poor and/or uneducated backgrounds, this advanced the reach and the academic credibility of JI's agenda. Even in the context of other university students, Azhari was highly educated, intelligent and sophisticated: an exemplary pickup for JI.

By 1998 it was clear to those spiritually close to him that Azhari had the intention of waging a vicious Jihad. However, he didn't yet have the capacity to do so; that needed to be rectified. With thousands of members in its ranks, JI was not short of those willing to assist with attacks. Their deficit was in technical bomb-making expertise. In response, the JI leadership saw fit to vault Azhari over more senior members and to fast-track his training and development.

While overseas training was being arranged for him, Azhari was actively talent-spotting for JI amongst his students at UTM. While maintaining a low religious and political profile, he befriended those that he considered to have a radical propensity. Once a level of trust had been established, he'd refer them to the LHIS to attend religious night lectures. There Mukhlas and his staff would preach strict Islamic values and Sharia law, encouraging the candidate towards more radical thinking. If the students continued down the pathway, and were considered an asset to JI, they would eventually take the organisational oath of allegiance.

To disguise his new life, Azhari continued to attend professional development seminars in Singapore and Jakarta, and published several academic articles on real estate market modelling and analysis.[35] Adhering strictly to the pledge he made, Azhari was extremely careful to maintain his cover and hide his radical views. For example, he purposefully avoided wearing a skullcap or Islamic robes, preferring to wear Western-style clothes, symbolising him as a modern broad-minded Muslim. He also shaved regularly, which under Sunni law is forbidden, unless it is part of a strategy against the infidel – which was exactly what he was doing.[36]

MILF

Azhari's strategy also successfully fooled Muslims on campus. One of his past students would later state,

> I cannot believe he is a terrorist. He always taught us to be a good person. There is no indication that he was involved in terrorist activities. He never showed that he was an extremist.[37]

Off campus too, his disguise was convincing. According to his neighbours at the time, 'There was no sign of radicalism in Azhari, or cruelty. Everybody was deceived with his calm demeanour and his cleverness in hiding his emotion.'[38]

Azhari deliberately projected a laissez-faire attitude in conversations where religion and politics were discussed and camouflaged his lethal religious hatred with benign statements such as 'Islam is a religion of peace'. But it clearly *wasn't* for Azhari – not anymore.

During the months that followed, Azhari used the library resources at UTM to research chemical engineering, electronics and physics. He also helped himself to a large array of laboratory equipment and chemical stores from the university, which he used to create his own research laboratory in the garage of his house. Azhari became infatuated with improving the effectiveness of explosive chemical reactions using domestically available ingredients that he knew would be available to him anywhere, anytime.

While Azhari read and researched, Nur Aini's voice gradually deteriorated to the point where she relied upon a notebook to communicate. She had long given up asking what her husband was doing. He either wouldn't answer her, or would simply say he was working. Azhari was preoccupied to the point that he had almost completely withdrawn from his family and social life. While he lived with Nur Aini and their two children, Azhari was really living by himself. Just as he had at university in Malaysia and the UK, he was now obsessed with achieving a goal. However, unlike his PhD, this goal went beyond the theoretical. Azhari now had a thirst to see the practical application of his newfound knowledge.

He didn't have to wait long.

Weeks later, Azhari was sitting on a crowded bus snaking its way through the mountains of Mindanao in the Southern Philippines. Mukhlas and Hambali had arranged funding and safe passage for Azhari deep into the volatile region controlled by the Moro Islamic Liberation Front (MILF).

For years MILF and other radical Muslim groups had been fighting the Philippine government for an Islamic state in the region.[39] MILF was then, and still is today, an organised and barbaric Islamic army with over 10,000 members. MILF had been responsible for multiple bomb attacks, beheadings,

MILF

executions and kidnappings of tourists to achieve their objectives. Hambali knew that MILF, as a result of its decades of violent Jihad, had a wealth of bomb-making experience that Azhari could learn and import to JI.

MILF's training facility, Camp Abubakar, was a centre for excellence in terrorist tactics and provided training to several international organisations. The facilities were vast and well protected. With a view to sending an increasing number of JI operatives for training, JI leadership would later broker a deal allowing JI to create their own training camp within Camp Abubakar, referred to as Camp Hudaibiyah.

The sheer magnitude of the operation in the Southern Philippines would have been an impressive eye-opener for Azhari, as would have been the students, who were nationally and racially diverse; yet all had the same violent goals. Azhari no doubt realised he was training to become part of a truly global Jihad. Azhari spent about four weeks in the camp, learning subjects such as bomb-making theory, bomb assembly, shrapnel techniques, effective bomb placement and so on. His natural aptitude, eye for detail and devotion to the subject would have been abundantly clear to the staff running the course, particularly when he shared the findings of his own research. Most of the bombs constructed by MILF relied on military high-grade explosives and some agricultural ingredients such as fertiliser and diesel. Conversely, Azhari's formulas relied on ostensibly domestically available cleaning products. He'd focused on using these types of products because, unlike C4 and TNT, they would be available in most locations and could be combined quickly by anyone who knew the formula.

The Indonesian police later confirmed his ability when they stated, 'He is an expert in mixing low and high explosives into something more powerful than a conventional bomb.'[40]

Months prior to Azhari attending the MILF course, Osama bin Laden had invited several radical groups to join the World Islamic Front to strengthen ties and coordinate their efforts in the 'religious war' against everyone that wasn't Muslim. Accepting the invitation, Sungkar and Bashir met directly with Osama bin Laden who, true to the Islamofascist agenda, had the ultimate goal of globalisation of the Islamic faith. He said to them:

> If the Arabian Peninsula, as the origin of Islam *(masdaru diinil Islam)* and the land's holiest place is successfully liberated, both its land and its wealth [can be released] from the grip of the American unbeliever, then God willing it will be able to smooth the struggle to uphold the Islamic faith all over Allah's Earth ...[41]

This message was in line with Jamaah Islamiyah's goals of, first, ridding Southeast Asia of non-believers (by killing or

MILF

converting them) and, second, to extend the Jihad into other countries until the supremacy of Islam prevailed.

The meeting strengthened the already close ties the two organisations had through bin Laden's relationship with Hambali, and increased JI's training opportunities in Afghanistan. In 1999, after his MILF training, this led to Azhari being sent on a bomb-training course with the Taliban in Kandahar, Afghanistan.

The Taliban advanced training courses centred, amongst other things, on the use of electronic triggering circuits. This would have introduced Azhari to innovative ways to detonate bombs using mobile phones, garage remote controls and even a car's central locking system. These techniques significantly complemented his already encyclopaedic knowledge and his almost photographic memory, which gave him the capacity to recall chemical formulations and electronic circuitry with astounding accuracy.

When Azhari returned to Malaysia it was clear he wanted to impart his newfound knowledge and ensure it was shared throughout JI. To do this, he used his university laptop to author a 50-page detailed bomb-making manual. The comprehensive document took considerable time for him to write. It included diagrams and step-by-step written instructions on surveillance methods when scouting for locations to bomb, explosive chemical formulations, a variety of electronic and physical triggering devices and effective bomb placement to maximise material and human destruction. Copies of the document, which became highly prized in terrorist networks, were later recovered by the Indonesian police from JI members and eventually from Azhari's own laptop.

While Azhari was toiling away on his laptop, Sungkar and Bashir migrated back to Indonesia. They returned because they expected that the new president, Habibie, would relax the crackdown on Muslim radicals, allowing JI to flourish, albeit under the government's radar. After returning to Ngruki from their self-imposed exile, they once again took over the day-to-day running of the Al-Mukmin *pesantren* and the strategic oversight of several other radical schools.

Despite the continued government crackdown and the absence of JI's two founding members over the previous several years, Al-Mukmin had continued to produce some dangerous alumni. The Al-Mukmin model had by now spread its tentacles and its ideology through more than 20 Islamic boarding schools.

By late 1999, Sungkar and Bashir were well on their way to achieving their goal of radicalising an entire generation when Sungkar suddenly suffered a fatal heart attack. Prior to his death, Sungkar had shared the spiritual leadership and guidance of JI with Bashir. While Sungkar was most definitely a fire-breathing religious bigot, he was sometimes also a voice of reason in Bashir's ear. With Sungkar dead, Bashir took over as the sole emir of JI.

MILF

Now under Bashir's unalloyed guidance were at least 20 Islamic boarding schools shaping the minds of susceptible children, and over 3000 graduates of Indonesian and Malaysian *pesantren*. The ultimate goal was to radicalise an entire generation. Critically, he also now had direct access to Osama bin Laden and Al-Qaeda resources through Hambali, a vastly increased training capacity in the newly created JI training facility with MILF, and Azhari – one of the most astute bomb makers ever to carry a Koran.

The stage was now set for an unrestrained, bloody Jihad.

MEANWHILE, BACK IN AUSTRALIA ...

2 October 2005

About 5.30 pm, I slid the ream of classified documents back inside the red satchel. This must've caught the watchful eye of the vault employee, who sprang to life and padlocked the satchel.

'Is that everything we've got on Jamaah Islamiyah?' I asked as he was about to leave.

'No, that's just Part One, up to the year 2000. I can bring you Part Two if you'd like.'

'That'd be great.'

'Also, there's been a lot of overseas intelligence reporting coming in during the day, because of what's happened in Bali. We usually compile each day's intelligence by 8 pm, so it's ready for the bosses in the morning. If you want to see the new stuff tonight, I could bring it up when it's been put together?' he said helpfully.

MEANWHILE, BACK IN AUSTRALIA ...

'Thanks, as soon as you have it please.'

Carrying me through the turmoil of the first IDETF and the senior executive briefings during the morning had been a basic understanding of the organisational history and of the major JI players. While I had definitely been thrown into the deep end with the magnitude of an international counterterrorism investigation, I considered myself a good swimmer. Realistically though, but for the support and tactical knowledge of those working for me, I could have drowned.

It was approaching 20 hours since I'd received the first phone call in Cairns. Thankfully, during that time I'd had a constant flow of verbal briefings from people with far more terrorist knowledge than I had at the time, which enabled me to keep my head above water. Now, having read Part One of the intelligence package, I realised just how much I still needed to know.

Countering my knowledge deficit was an abundance of determination to see those responsible for the killings held accountable. I owed that to the victims. I knew I'd need to rely upon a cocktail of adrenaline, my sense of professional responsibility and a near-intravenous supply of caffeine to get me through what would end up being a 31-hour shift, followed by multiple consecutive 16- to 20-hour work days.

Throughout the afternoon and into the night, the information from the Forward Command Post in Bali and the

DEFEATING TERROR

Incident Coordination Centre (ICC) in Canberra flowed fast and furious. A primary source of this was the 5000 passengers who were interviewed by the airport investigation teams as they returned from Bali. The Australian public were very helpful in this regard, with most completing written questionnaires, others volunteering information verbally and some providing all their holiday photos and videos as possible evidence.

Conducting so many interviews in such a short time is a double-edged sword. On one side, it's highly likely you will get very accurate contemporaneous information from people, but the other side of the blade is that some, even those who witnessed the events first-hand, are completely inaccurate and misleading. It's an unfortunate consequence when people witness a truly shocking incident: it can sometimes play tricks on their mind and facts can be distorted. Both edges of the sword were presenting themselves to the airport investigation teams.

I received copies of firsthand reports from witnesses in the same location that observed the same thing, and yet their recollection of the same incident drastically conflicted with each other. For example, some eyewitnesses from Jimbaran Bay reported that they had seen the explosions burst from the sand under the tables at the restaurants. Even one of the Australian witnesses sitting at the Newcastle table that night verified this account.[42] Others 'saw' the attackers throw a package under the

MEANWHILE, BACK IN AUSTRALIA ...

Newcastle table before running away unscathed. Two witnesses from Raja's said they saw the offender place a bomb on the bar at the back of the restaurant before running to the safety of the street. Another saw a person throw a white package from the street into the restaurant seconds before the blast.

In hindsight, it's easy to rule out such accounts. But, at the time all information had to be considered possible until corroborated or discounted through reliable investigative or forensic procedures. Every lead had to be tracked down. In counterterrorism investigations, the stakes are too high to simply make an assessment and dismiss information. If you get it wrong, people die.

So investigate we did. Very few counterterrorism members in Australia and Bali, AFP and INP, got much sleep as we chased every rabbit down every hole and ran down every lead to its end. That's not to say there weren't knowledge gaps. As is often the case in major crime investigations, when a magnifying glass is finely applied to a line of enquiry, it will produce three or four new leads that then need to be resolved.

Quickly adding to the complexity of the investigation were multiple independent witness accounts of people receiving SMS messages or being warned verbally in advance of the bombings. None of this information could be discounted either, and some of the information appeared to be very accurate, including a group of 14 Australians from Brisbane who reported they had been forewarned of the bombing by security staff at the Hard Rock Hotel.[43]

Confounding things further, the day after the bombing a new SMS message was being rapidly circulated in Indonesia foretelling of another bomb expected in Bali. One of the messages was,

> Police Intel Bali: got information that can be next
> bomb in some place around JI. Please be careful, pass to
> everyone u know to avoid any problem in next few days.[44]

The prime minister, John Howard, instructed the AFP to investigate these claims. This too landed on my desk. When his referral to the AFP was made public, several new text messages were transmitted warning of different times and places for the expected bombs. None of these could be discounted until they were disproven. If one of these messages was proven to be correct, even by coincidence, and people were killed or injured, the ramifications for the AFP, and ultimately me, not to have been actively pursuing those lines of enquiry were enormous, not to mention the deaths that may have been prevented. Every rabbit down every hole.

At the time of the bombings, JI was not listed as a terrorist organisation in Indonesia. It was not banned or restricted in any way. So, membership, fundraising, financing, gathering

MEANWHILE, BACK IN AUSTRALIA ...

and other organised activities were not themselves illegal although they were still carried out covertly. Prime Minister Howard had previously urged Indonesian President Susilo Bambang Yudhoyono to ban the organisation, but this had been opposed.[45] Had JI been banned, not only would it have made it more difficult for the organisation to flourish over the preceding decade, it would have assisted with the investigation into events such as these bombings – if at the time we definitely knew JI was behind the attacks.

Multiple media reports were quick to finger JI and Azhari for the attacks. This was understandable considering the history of bombings in Southeast Asia. However, the information in the first intelligence package I had just read, particularly around bomb construction and attack techniques, conflicted with some of these early reports coming from Bali that the bombs were either thrown into the restaurants, buried beneath the restaurant tables or carried in backpacks by suicide bombers. These techniques weren't mainstays of either MILF or Taliban training, both of which Azhari had attended. To remain objective I couldn't be influenced and needed to rely solely upon known facts and reliable intelligence. At this stage I needed to remain open to the possibility that the attack was *not* carried out by Azhari.

I desperately needed Part Two of the JI Intelligence Package, which covered 2000 to 2005 – I was particularly interested in JI's most recent attack methodologies. Learning this would allow me to do a comparative analysis between those attacks and the conflicting circumstances of the bombings. That would take me some way to either ruling the organisation and its membership in or out of the investigation focus. JI was not the only terrorist group active in Southeast Asia, so, despite what the media were saying on the first day, it was far from a foregone conclusion that JI had been involved.

From the outset, it was made clear there was a high expectation held by senior management that we should be able to identify the three suicide bombers and the network supporting them very quickly. Naively gung-ho, I felt confident that we could meet that expectation. The first Bali bombing took about three weeks before its first major breakthrough,[46] but since 2002 there had been joint INP–AFP active terrorist tracking teams in Indonesia and 125 JI radicals had been arrested.[47] As a result, there was a vast amount of intelligence about the network, its practices and its past methodologies; I'd just skimmed the surface.

Just after 8 pm, there was a knock on my door and another red satchel was placed on my desk, then unlocked and unzipped.

'Thanks,' I said, looking at the pregnant satchel.

'I'll just wait out here,' the young man said politely as he resumed his seat outside my office.

MEANWHILE, BACK IN AUSTRALIA ...

Without hesitation, I reached into the red lucky-dip bag and withdrew its contents. For a moment I stared at the two 3-centimetre-thick bound assemblages; one with 'TOP SECRET – AUSTEO' (Australian Eyes Only) and the other with 'TOP SECRET – FIVE EYES' (Australia, UK, US, Canada and New Zealand) stamped in bright-red ink at the top and bottom of the external cover and every page within each compendium.[48]

Together, these formed Part Two of the JI Intelligence Package. It contained the most recent compendium of the latest intelligence reports from police and intelligence agencies from around the world. I desperately hoped it would help me ascertain if Azhari, the prime suspect, was in fact behind the latest attack. However, there was something I didn't know, something no-one had noticed within the documentation: it was laced with Azhari's evolution as a killer.

PART TWO

THE EVOLUTION OF KILLING

A CRITICAL MASS

In February 2000, the crackling speakers of the Solo Mosque broadcast the call to prayer for the thousands of devoted Muslim men in the district. The faithful filed in through the gates of the ageing cream concrete walls that perimetered the football field-sized grounds. Dotted about the partially paved and flat dirt grounds were lampposts that had many years before been painted aquamarine, but were now, courtesy of the relentless Indonesian sun, a faded pastel blue. From the outside the Great Mosque and its surrounds were dilapidated.

The large crowd slowly queued to enter the cavernous main prayer hall. By contrast, it was the antithesis of the exterior. The floor was a layer of highly polished marble tiles, cleverly laid diagonally across the expansive area. The vaulted ceiling was an ascending trapezoid structure, formed by four colossal dark wood-ribbed walls that leaned towards each other. Midway along the pyramid roofline was a strip of glass ventilation windows that vacuumed out body heat and drew in fresh air through the wooden entry doors. Inside, hundreds of men in white cotton throbes formed neat parallel prayer lines between the monolithic wooden poles that soared from the floor to brace the majestic roof structure.

The vast majority of attendees that day were religiously dedicated and peaceful Muslims. However, disguised within the harmonious flock were malevolent Muslim wolves in the form of Hambali, Mukhlas and his two younger brothers: Amrozi and the recently battle-hardened Imron, who had just returned from fighting in Afghanistan. Completing the pack was Azhari, who had made the trip from Johor with electronic copies of the JI bomb-making manual and Imam Samudra, who had attended the LHIS where Mukhlas had sculpted him into a dedicated Jihadist.[49] Samudra, too, had just returned from Afghanistan smitten with bloodlust for a holy war and had brought his close Islamic school friend, Idris al-Gembrot (Idris), who would become a primary attack weapon for JI.[50]

The month before, Hambali, as Al-Qaeda's representative in Southeast Asia and chief of operations for JI, had hosted a vital planning meeting in Kuala Lumpur. It was a meeting where attacks were planned for US warships in the Middle East (present were bombers involved later that year with the attack on the USS *Cole*)[51] and the 9/11 attack plans for the United States were further developed (present were two of the 9/11 hijackers).

A CRITICAL MASS

After the prayers had concluded, the large crowd spilled out from the various exits onto the roughly paved grounds. Hambali silently led his pack to a secluded area of the grounds where they could talk out of others' earshot. Hambali didn't elaborate on the details of the meeting he had hosted in Kuala Lumpur, but he did tell the men that Al-Qaeda had a number of attack plans for other parts of the world, and that he wanted JI efforts to coincide with those of their Middle Eastern brothers.

To engineer this, Hambali had hatched an ambitious plan to convert or kill as many Christians as possible in Indonesia, with the preference being the latter. He explained to the group that their goal could be achieved quickly through an Indonesian holy war between Muslims and Christians; and it was just the strategy for JI to kickstart the conflict in three easy steps.

Step one: disseminate throughout the *usroh* network and as many other sources as possible the falsehood that Christians are preparing for a holy war and are storing firearms and explosives in their churches.

Step two: a group headed by Samudra will bomb 50 Christian churches. But not just *any* Christian churches: just selected ones in areas where the Christian community is significantly outnumbered by Muslims. Hambali's shallow rationale was based on the hypothesis that nonviolent Muslims would, having heard the rumours, understand that if Christians were storing weapons in churches, then those buildings were a legitimate

DEFEATING TERROR

target in defence of Islam. This was meant to attenuate any opposition to the attacks within the Muslim community.

Step three relied upon the assumption that, with so many churches being bombed, Christians would retaliate and attack mosques and Muslims. However, as the churches bombed were situated in areas where Christians were outnumbered, the Muslim community would have a significant advantage. A product of any retaliatory Christian attacks would be the religious obligation amongst Muslims to defend Islam. Thus, the whole community would band together to kill Christians. The Christians, being significantly outnumbered, would ultimately lose. A sadistically evil plan, brilliantly conceived to amplify hatred, division and fear. This was terrorism at its core.

Receiving little to no opposition to the plan, Hambali told the men he had timed the attack for Christmas Eve that year (2000), when the churches would be packed with worshippers.

Azhari was responsible for the design and construction of the majority of the bombs and would be assisted by other JI operatives with the construction. His eyes must have lit up when Hambali informed him that, through MILF, Hambali had arranged for 2 tonnes of ammonium nitrate (a highly effective explosive fertiliser) to be shipped from Mindanao in the Philippines to Poso in Central Sulawesi, Indonesia to use for the explosive mix. For the first time Azhari was a critical player in JI's biggest-ever bombing campaign.

A CRITICAL MASS

Over the next few months Samudra supervised the planning, logistics and reconnaissance of churches and priests' homes.[52] By November 2000, most of the electronic components and chemicals, including the ammonium nitrate fertiliser and TNT stolen from a tin mine, had been delivered to a number of locations. Azhari and his cohorts then commenced mixing 50 'cakes', as they affectionately called their bombs. Electronic components were judiciously soldered onto circuit boards and switches were carefully sown into bags and hidden in boxes, then connected to chemicals mixed according to Azhari's recipe.

Azhari had designed his devices so they were simple to use. All the bomber had to do was plug in a 9-volt battery, place the device for maximum effect and flick a single switch activating the timing circuit. Where possible Azhari advised that they were to place the bombs under the church pulpit, or under the building itself on a small square of bricks that they should place there. This way the explosion wouldn't be absorbed by the ground underneath it. Rather, it would be shaped and directed upwards and outwards, vastly increasing its lethal capacity. By the afternoon of 24 December 2000, the devices had been primed and delivered to 12 different cities.

Some of the devices were wired with a three-hour timing circuit so operatives would be able to use the cover of darkness, just after nightfall, to place and set the bombs, well before worshippers would arrive. Then three hours later the

DEFEATING TERROR

explosions would tear through the attending congregation in the middle of the 9 pm mass. Not only would this maximise human casualties, it would spread terror across the nation and prevent thousands from attending the traditional Christian midnight mass.

Some syndicate members elected to wire their devices with mobile phones instead of timing circuits. Enjang Bastaman (aka Jabir) in the JI Bandung group was one such member. He was working with five others in a car repair shop in Bandung (150 kilometres south-east of Jakarta) constructing four bombs in readiness for the attack. When he wired his phone to one of the bombs, he absentmindedly forgot to remove the SIM card. Later on Christmas Eve, as the group were diligently working together, someone attempted to phone him, triggering the bomb. It killed Jabir and three other group members. Two members, including the owner of the car repair shop, were injured and fled but were arrested the following day in Central Java.

In the Ciamis district (West Java) that Christmas Eve, parishioners were having dinner, ironing their clothes and preparing themselves to attend the church's most critical mass. Not far away, two JI operatives were also preparing to attend the church, but for a very different reason.

On a motor scooter, the pair set off towards the church when suddenly their lane in the rapid flow of traffic came to a stop, apparently catching the pair by surprise. As can occur in

Above: Australian Federal Police (AFP) investigate the site of the Marriott Hotel bomb blast in Jakarta in 2003 where a car bomb ripped through the Jakarta hotel. It contained the same cocktail of explosives as the Bali bombs in 2002 and was also detonated by a mobile phone. (STR/AFP/Getty Images)

Below: Indonesian Muslim cleric Abu Bakar Bashir being escorted to trial in Jakarta in November 2004. Bashir was accused of inciting followers to carry out both the October 2002 Bali bombing in which 202 people died and the attack on the Jakarta Marriott Hotel in which 12 were killed. (ADEK BERRY/AFP/Getty Images)

Above: A tourist's amateur video shows the moments leading up to the explosion that ripped through the Raja restaurant in Kuta, Bali, on 1 October 2005. (Getty Images)

Below: The video recorded the instant when the first suicide bomber detonated his backpack, fatally blasting ball-bearing schrapnel into the crowded restaurant. (Getty Images)

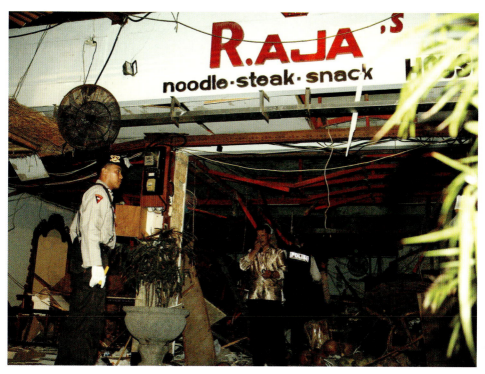

Above: Indonesian security personnel survey the scene at the bomb-damaged restaurant the day after it was hit by the suicide bomber. (STR/AFP/Getty Images)

Below: The site where Raja's Bar and Restaurant was bombed in 2005. The shopfront remains closed but the restaurant has relocated in Kuta and continues to be popular with tourists.

Above: Jimbaran beach restaurants are again full of people in 2017, just as they were in 2005 before Islamic extremists attacked.

Below: An Indonesian policeman sets up a cordon around the bomb blast site on Jimbaran beach. (JEWEL SAMAD/AFP/Getty Images)

AFP and Indonesian forensic officers collect evidence from the bomb site outside the Nyoman Cafe on Jimbaran beach. (JASON CHILDS/Getty Images)

Below: Newspapers depict police at work inside one of the restaurants in their search for clues. Also pictured are the suspects behind the bombings: Jemaah Islamiyah members Abu Bakar Bashir, Noordin Top and Dr Azhari Husin.

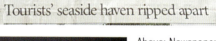

Above: Newspaper reports follow the hunt for the Bali bombers.

Left: Detective Superintendent David Craig headed the AFP counter-terrorism investigation into the 2005 Bali bombings.

Above: A local resident shows a poster featuring the ghoulish pictures of the three suicide bombers. He is standing next to some of the wreckage on Jimbaran beach, the site of the 1 October 2005 bombings in Bali. (JEWEL SAMAD/AFP/Getty Images)

Police put up a new poster showing reconstructed images of the suspects, offering a reward of 100 million rupiah (10,000 USD) for information leading to their identification. (BAY ISMOYO/AFP/Getty Images)

Above: At sunset, the bombers prayed behind this building and then waited out of sight until the appointed time to set off on their deadly attacks.

Below: The presidential suite at the Kartika Plaza Hotel, Kuta, was used by AFP and INP as a base to investigate the Bali bombings both in 2002 and in 2005.

A CRITICAL MASS

these situations on a motorcycle, it appears the rider instinctively grabbed a handful of front brake, causing the front tyre to skid and the front end of the scooter to give way and the pair to slide into the vehicle in front. In a nanosecond, the 9-volt electrical pulse ignited the TNT, which instantaneously combusted about 5 kilograms of ammonium nitrate. The savage burst of energy shredded the flesh from the bones of the two men and sent a hail of razor-sharp shrapnel and blood mist through the surrounding vehicles.

Over the next few hours, hundreds of unsuspecting Christian worshippers would fill their churches to capacity, oblivious to the JI juggernaut that was coming their way.

By about 7 pm that night, JI operatives had placed bombs in, under or next to 47 churches and family homes of Christian priests and ministers in 11 Indonesian cities. Hambali's group were confident they had set the stage to initiate a religious war where Christians would retaliate after the bombings and be outnumbered and slaughtered by the larger Muslim community.

Even in the context of barbaric Islamic extremism, those involved in targeting the Eben Haezer church in Mojokerto (East Java) had a particularly venomous approach. After placing a device inside the church, a second device with its timing circuit set to a later time was placed next to a public phone near the front of the building with the view to killing worshippers who fled the church after the first bomb exploded.

By 9.30 pm, well after the time set for the explosions, the Eben Haezer church service was continuing uninterrupted. Those who had placed the bombs, and were most likely observing from afar, would have realised both devices had malfunctioned. However, at that juncture there would have been very little they could do to remedy the situation; attempting to retrieve either device would increase their risk of discovery and arrest, or the device detonating unexpectedly.

After the service concluded, one of the congregation, Banser Nu Riyanto, a middle-aged office worker who had attended the mass with his wife and three children, noticed a bag next to the public phone. After unzipping it Riyanto immediately knew what it was and shouted a warning to the rest of the crowd emerging from the church.

As panic swept through the congregation, Riyanto gingerly carried the dangerous cargo step by step for about 10 metres to the edge of a flowing cement sewerage channel. Then, he gently lobbed the backpack into the flowing effluent. On impact the bomb detonated, tearing Riyanto's body to pieces, killing him instantly. The shock wave shattered shop windows up to a kilometre away. Riyanto's wife fainted with the shock of seeing her husband reduced to a charred mass of flesh and bone on the grass. Elsewhere in Indonesia, 25 bombs were successfully detonated in churches and priests' homes, killing 20 people and seriously injuring over 120 others.

A CRITICAL MASS

In the days that followed, the JI operation would be viewed as an epic failure by Hambali and his Al-Qaeda puppetmaster for two primary reasons. First, rather than divide the Christian and Muslim communities, the attacks on churches were criticised by Muslim leaders and strengthened the solidarity between the two communities, particularly as it became evident that weapons were not found in any churches. Secondly, with only 50 per cent of the bombs successfully detonating, Azhari had some explaining to do.

Still believing the Christian community would eventually retaliate, members of the group commenced sporadic shooting attacks on Christian community leaders, resulting in another three deaths. Following this, two Christian schoolgirls were beheaded and their decapitated bodies were left at the front of their church. Still no uprising – still a one-sided holy war.

Hambali's plan had tactical success in that it killed Christians. However, as there was no violent Christian retaliation, there was nothing to inspire the broader Muslim community to stand united in a holy war against the Christians – strategically it had been a spectacular failure. While Hambali carried this heavy burden, it would have been nothing compared to the one that Azhari was laden with. The failure of so many devices no doubt dented both his pride and his credibility as *the* JI bomb expert.

Over the following weeks, Azhari must have spent many hours sifting through his notes and assessing the successful

91

detonations and the failures. At some point during that process, he diagnosed the problem. All the bombs that successfully detonated had the electronic circuitry enclosed in Tupperware-type containers. The devices that failed to explode had the trigger circuitry inside small cardboard boxes. The bomb construction design he had used was one he had learned at the training camp in Kandahar, Afghanistan. The fighting season in Afghanistan commences in spring and continues through the hot, dry, dusty months. As such, the design didn't require protection from moisture. It was a very different case in Indonesia, where the country's humidity wrought havoc on the electronic components that were not sealed from the elements.

This was a defining moment in Azhari's bomb design development. From that point onwards, he would construct very reliable plug-in modular bombs with sections sealed inside plastic containers to protect them from moisture. This became one of Azhari's bomb signatures that would be found in over 200 bombs.[53]

His evolution as a killer had begun.

NO PLACE FOR FAMILY

After the Christmas Eve attacks, Azhari returned to Malaysia, where he resumed lecturing at the UTM in Johor. Unlike the majority of lecturers, Azhari had always been careful to wear Westernised clothing, specifically to project a peaceful guise and to hide his increasingly fanatical views. According to one student, 'Azhari had stood out in contrast to other Muslim lecturers by the lack of such overt symbolism like wearing the "Haji" skullcaps or Middle Eastern robes.'[54] No doubt this was a deliberate ploy to stay below the sweep of intelligence agencies' radars that in Malaysia were finally focusing upon radicalism.

If Azhari believed wearing Western-style clothing projected that he was a more moderate Muslim, then logically when he was talent-spotting for JI recruits at UTM he would have targeted students clad in Middle Eastern clothes, based on the assumption they were either more radical, or had a

93

DEFEATING TERROR

radical predisposition. One such student was Noor Din bin Mohammed Top, a Malaysian national. Top was quick to learn and shared Azhari's passion and propensity for religious violence. The pair quickly formed a kinship of trust; Azhari had found his protege.

In an effort to coordinate JI's spread of Islamofascism, Hambali, in consultation with Bashir and Sungkar, had geographically divided Asia into four areas of responsibility, called *Mantiqis*. Each *Mantiqi* came under the command of an appointed regional leadership council, each reporting to Hambali.

Mantiqi One covered Malaysia and Singapore. Its responsibility was to raise funds from the wealthy businesses in the region. *Mantiqi* Two covered Indonesia and its responsibility was to establish an Islamic state through Jihad. *Mantiqi* Three covered East Kalimantan, Sulawesi and southern Philippines, and was responsible for training. The other *Mantiqi* covered Papua and Australia; its responsibility was to assist financing operations.[55] Hambali, who was the linchpin to coordinate with, sought funding from Al-Qaeda, remained as overall chief of operations for the entire region and nominated himself the leader of *Mantiqi* One (Malaysia and Singapore).

In June 2000, Hambali called a meeting in Johor for key members of his *Mantiqi*, including Azhari, Top and the three brothers Mukhlas, Amrozi and Imron, who were by then all teaching at the LHIS. It's possible that it was at that meeting

NO PLACE FOR FAMILY

that Top took the JI oath of allegiance and formally joined JI's ranks. No doubt the failure of the Christmas Eve bombings strategy would have been discussed. Far from sparking a holy war, it had brought the Muslim and Christian communities closer together. Making things worse, immediately after the bombings Christian leaders told the Indonesian media that they had already forgiven the bombers.

This must have been puzzling behaviour to the war-mongering JI leadership. Equally puzzling would have been the fact that they were losing support within the Muslim community, rather than inspiring others to join the Jihad. Either way, it would have been clear that it was pointless to continue attacking in the same way. Change was needed; that was the purpose of Hambali's call.

Hambali had just travelled to Singapore, Malaysia and the Philippines with an Al-Qaeda affiliate to review operations and to discuss the change in direction.[56] Hambali's solution was to attack American, Israeli and British embassies in Singapore.[57] Spiritual approval for the attacks had been provided, most likely by Bashir, and funding arranged through Al-Qaeda. As the plan developed, the Australian High Commission in Singapore was also included as a target. This may well have been a result of Azhari's urgings, or the promulgation of ill-informed terrorist propaganda concerning Australia's involvement with East Timor at the time, or a combination of both.

DEFEATING TERROR

In 2000, many militants believed that Australia had led a Christian crusade under the guise of the United Nations to take over the 'Muslim land' of East Timor. This misinformation discounted the fact that it was a series of UN Security Council resolutions that authorised 22 countries, including predominantly Muslim countries, to intervene in the East Timorese crisis.[58]

It also discounted the historic fact that, apart from Japanese occupation for a short period during World War II, the Christian Portuguese had colonised and administered the country for over 400 years and the vast majority of the population were Christian. The propaganda didn't mention that East Timor was invaded by Indonesian troops just nine days after they declared themselves independent from Portugal in 1975. That was when they became Indonesian – the population's religion didn't change, just their nationality.

The inconvenient truth was that East Timor had been a predominantly Christian country for over four centuries. Regardless of the inaccuracies, the rumour found traction amongst quick-to-hate and ignorant terrorists who remained convinced there was a holy war over land. Bin Laden would later release a tape to the Al Jazeera news network attesting to this, in which he specifically mentions Australia as a legitimate terror target for taking over the 'Muslim' country of East Timor.[59] Irrespective of the reasoning behind the decision, there is little doubt that Azhari would have been very satisfied that Australia was now in the crosshairs of both JI and Al-Qaeda.

Traditional and video footage reconnaissance (that would later be released to the public) of the targets in Singapore, including the Australian High Commission, was hastily completed.[60] Following this, Azhari, assisted by other JI bomb-makers, listed their requirements for a successful mission.[61] After the failure of so many devices during the Christmas Eve attacks, little was being left to chance. The attack would be of a magnitude that had never been attempted before in Southeast Asia. The apocalyptic campaign required 17 tonnes of ammonium nitrate and 9 tonnes of TNT. It required truck bombs to be constructed in one of the MILF training camps in the Philippines, where their construction could be better hidden from the authorities.[62] It was estimated it would take about 12 months to fully prepare for the attack, which was to be launched in December 2001.

On 11 September 2001, Al-Qaeda launched its shocking and cowardly attacks on the US. To Muslim radicals, though, it was seen as anything but shocking and cowardly. It was a time to celebrate and rejoice. Hypocritically, televisions that were banned by Sharia law were suddenly okay to watch, as were the videotaped replays. Exceptions were also made in some of the *pesantren*, so children could observe and enjoy what was considered a great victory.

In response to the 9/11 attacks, the US accused Afghanistan's ruling power, the Taliban, of protecting Al-Qaeda's leader, Osama bin Laden. On 7 October 2001, the US launched Operation Enduring Freedom and attacked Taliban bases and training camps. In November 2001, US Special Forces in Afghanistan located hundreds of paper and electronic files. One of these files was the detailed bombing plan for Singapore and the related surveillance footage. Days later, the US shared this intelligence with the Singaporean and Malaysian governments.

On 18 December 2001, about 11.30 pm, according to Nur Aini, Azhari walked into the family house and appeared confused and anxious. As he proceeded to pace back and forth in the house, he said to Nur Aini, 'I feel like the police are chasing me. Many of my friends have been arrested. But I don't want to be captured.'[63]

This was very confusing for Nur Aini, who on her account had no idea why the police would be interested in her husband. Nur Aini would later recount in an interview that the pair had then lain in bed together restlessly until around 1.30 am, when she fell asleep. A short time later, when she woke, Azhari was gone. She desperately searched outside the house and used what little was left of her voice to call out to him – but there was no reply.

The following night, Nur Aini found a note from Azhari:

NO PLACE FOR FAMILY

I am very sorry for leaving abruptly. Actually, I love
my wife and my children. But, I have to go to work on
something. Protect the kids. Teach them good morals. I
want you to be patient with this test. Remember, Muslims
cannot be weak and lose hope.[64]

On finding the note, Nur Aini's greatest fears must have been
realised. The man she loved was a terrorist. And he had left her
alone to continue her fight with throat cancer and to raise their
two young children with no income.

In Azhari's killing evolution, there was no place for family.

JIMI'S CAKE

On 18 December 2001, acting on the US intelligence retrieved from Afghanistan, the Singaporean authorities arrested 15 JI members for their involvement with the embassy bombing plot and detained 34 more for questioning. The Malaysian police acted decisively too, arresting several known JI members around Kuala Lumpur just hours after Azhari had fled.

News of the arrests spread quickly through the JI network, causing a rapid human exodus from Malaysia. Amrozi and Imron left Johor about 2.30 am and returned to Central Java, Indonesia. Mukhlas, taking with him $14,000 of *Mantiqi* One money, similarly fled the LHIS. By the time Azhari and Top were crossing the border from Malaysia to southern Thailand on a bus, Malaysian authorities were raiding their houses and the administration offices at LHIS. Intelligence sources correctly identified the LHIS as a hive of JI recruitment and radical Muslim teachings. The Malaysian government closed the school. It was never reopened.

JIMI'S CAKE

After lying low for a few weeks, Hambali hosted a meeting in Southern Thailand in January 2002 with Mukhlas, Samudra, Azhari and Top.[65] Hambali knew he was being actively hunted by the Americans for his involvement with the 9/11 attacks and was aware that the Indonesian and Malaysian governments were also seeking his whereabouts. So he had his hair cut short, changed the shape of his facial hair and rarely wore his trademark glasses. Despite having changed his appearance and having used his new false passport under the name 'Hendrawan' to fly to Thailand from Indonesia, Hambali figured his days were numbered.[66] In a move to ensure JI business continuity if he was arrested, Hambali handed operational leadership of JI to Mukhlas. This decision was supported unanimously by the group.

Despite having fought Jihad in Afghanistan and run the LHIS that successfully mind-altered many children into radical Islamic thinking, this sudden promotion must have come as a shock to Mukhlas. He had assumed command of about 3000 JI members during a particularly turbulent time.

In the wake of 9/11 and the US's aggressive pursuit of those responsible, it would have been understandable for the group to lead JI into an operational hiatus and allow the storm to pass over. However, that wasn't their thinking. It was decided that embassies were no longer viable targets as most had been hardened by increased security measures. So another strategy change was required. Now, the focus moved to soft targets such as businesses, tourist spots and nightclubs. Mukhlas was responsible for taking JI into this new cowardly domain.

In response to 9/11, several governments had frozen Al-Qaeda bank accounts and the enabling finances of other terrorist organisations. However, in addition to the $14,000 Mukhlas had taken from the LHIS, Hambali had arranged (through Al-Qaeda) to receive $30,000 cash towards the next JI attack, which he would later forward to Mukhlas.[67]

Over the next few days, most likely using fake identification documents, all the men except Hambali, who was frightened by the prospect of being discovered by the CIA at a border crossing, returned to Indonesia undetected. Mukhlas returned to his home village of Tenggulun and met with his two younger brothers, Amrozi and Imron. The trio discussed in detail the change in strategy and it was decided that the Hindu island of Bali was the ideal location for the next major attack.

To conduct reconnaissance as a tourist, rather than a terrorist, Imron travelled by ferry to Bali where he booked into a small apartment in Denpasar. There he was later joined by Samudra, who had been nominated as the commander of the Bali attack. From their fundamentalist Islamic perspective, the men would have been shocked at what they saw in Bali compared to the traditional Islamic communities they had

JIMI'S CAKE

grown up in. Surveying the scene they would have observed men drinking alcohol and women walking alone in public and wearing shorts and shirts exposing their hair, arms and legs; Kuta would have looked like nothing more than a cesspit of Kafirs (nonbelievers). No doubt they believed they were targeting the correct island.

Their reconnaissance focused upon several places, including the open-air Sari Club. The club itself was essentially a large cement square with thatched pergolas that covered the bars and dance floor. It was fronted with a low iron-paling fence along the footpath, which allowed the men to see the activities inside the club. As it did every night, the Sari Club would have had music pumping out of its speakers encouraging men in singlets and women wearing shorts, and even shorter skirts, onto the dance floor. With a crowd of foreign people dancing, laughing and openly drinking alcohol, to the radical observers the site was packed with filth and immorality. In their survey report, Samudra and Imron noted that many of the men had short haircuts, which they mistakenly thought indicated they were American military personnel, when in fact they were Australian rugby players. They concluded that the Sari Club was a target-rich environment. Following the reconnaissance trip, there were a series of JI meetings, including at a Solo mosque and Bashir's house in Solo, where he gave a large amount of cash towards funding the soft-target bombing campaign.[68]

DEFEATING TERROR

In August 2002, Mukhlas called the key players together for a critical planning meeting. Those who attended included his two younger brothers, Amrozi and Imron. Also present was Samudra, fellow Christmas Eve bomber Idris, and JI newcomer Dulmatin, who had just been freshly trained by Azhari in bomb-making.[69] Mukhlas announced that he had confirmation from Bashir that the use of martyrs was religiously legitimate under Islamic law and in accordance with the Koran. As such, Bashir had given his blessing for the use of suicide bombers. This was unprecedented in Southeast Asia.

This decision would change the entire attack philosophy for Bali. Rather than simply place bombs, as they had with the Christmas Eve attacks, a suicide bomber could take the device anywhere at any time they needed, and could personally detonate the bomb at the best time, rather than relying on timing circuits and remote detonating. This was a great practical advantage and it added the religious legitimacy of martyrdom. After the Christmas Eve bombings, many in the Muslim community spoke out against their actions. This time, the men may have expected other Muslims would understand that they were defending Muslim lands from the immoral Kafirs who were invading Bali.

The date decided for the Bali bombing was September 11, to commemorate the Al-Qaeda attacks on that day 12 months earlier, and to show the world that JI was part of the global Jihad

JIMI'S CAKE

to Islamise the world. However, during the preparation phase it became apparent that it would not be practically possible to meet the September 11 deadline, so the date was changed to 12 October 2002. This was the day in 2000 when their Muslim brothers attacked the American destroyer USS *Cole* in Yemen, killing 17 US personnel and injuring 39 others. It was certainly a date to celebrate and also to pay homage to their previous commander, Hambali, who had been directly involved with planning that attack.

After the August meeting, the men dispersed to concentrate on their allocated tasks. Two weeks later, Amrozi, assisted by Idris, bought a white 1983 Mitsubishi L300 van to serve as the main bomb platform.[70] The pair drove the van to his home village of Tenggulun in East Java. Amrozi immediately set to work on the vehicle, removing the seats and installing a flat false wooden floor in the back to make it easier to mount the 1-tonne bomb. To avoid the van being traced to him after the bombing, Amrozi used an angle grinder to grind off the engine and chassis numbers.

On 18 September 2002, Amrozi was satisfied the van was ready: now all he needed to do was purchase the ammonium nitrate fertiliser. He drove into Surabaya on that day and again on 23 September, each time purchasing about 500 kilograms of explosive fertiliser mix from the Tidar Kimia chemical shop; a place where he had bought fertiliser for the same purpose previously. Despite the chemicals not being prohibited, Amrozi insisted the receipt be written out for a different type of chemical, again to distance himself from any subsequent investigation into the attack.

On 25 September 2002, Samudra visited Amrozi and Idris in Tenggulun to see how they were progressing. He was impressed with what he saw and ordered that the explosives be sent in 50-kilogram packages by bus from Surabaya to Bali. After Samudra left, Idris caught a bus from Surabaya to Bali. Over the following days, Amrozi packaged up and sent a multitude of 50-kilogram boxes of ammonium nitrate, potassium chlorate, sulphur, TNT and aluminium powder by bus. Idris duly collected all the packages and stashed them at a rented house at 18 Manjangan Street, in Denpasar, Bali.

By 5 October all the packages had been collected, so Amrozi and Imron left Tenggulun in the L300 van. They picked up Dulmatin, who brought several boxes of bomb componentry, including detonator cord and electronic circuits disguised in cigarette cartons. On their way to Bali they purchased 12 plastic four-drawer cabinets to use as the bomb casing.

The three men arrived in Bali about 11 pm on 6 October and checked into the Hotel Harum in Denpasar. By this time, it appears Samudra had lost confidence in Dulmatin and the others to construct the bombs successfully, so he summoned Azhari to Bali.

JIMI'S CAKE

The final major planning meeting occurred just two days later when Mukhlas, Samudra, Amrozi, Imron, Idris, Dulmatin and Azhari met at 18 Manjangan Street.[71] The rundown two-level terrace house was nestled between two larger houses that it shared adjoining walls with. Access to the house was through a rusty iron lace fence that lined most of the houses on the narrow one-way road as it snaked its way through the poor suburb. The Mitsubishi L300 was parked in the small carport at the side of the roughly concreted front yard.

Inside, the meagrely furnished house had plain concrete floors and lime-washed walls. While it was inadequately ventilated through small windows, it provided the privacy they needed for their bomb factory. The room was scattered with the boxes couriered from Surabaya, plastic filing cabinets, several drums of various chemicals and an array of hand tools ranging from drills to large aluminium baker's mixing bowls. Azhari, assisted by others, was assigned to supervise the biggest 'cake' JI had ever mixed.[72]

To meet the 12 October deadline, over the next few days Azhari and his team worked at a frenetic pace. The living room would have looked like a bakehouse, with empty 50-kilogram sacks on one side of the room and, on the other, diligent bakers carefully mixing various coloured powders in large bowls. Azhari, the chief baker, would have been systematically weighing the ingredients, then monitoring as the team methodically and carefully mixed the volatile recipe.

DEFEATING TERROR

At the end of the production line sat 48 large plastic drawers. After the chief baker had quality-assured each 25-kilogram batch of powder, it was poured delicately into a drawer. That drawer was then carefully inserted into its place in a filing cabinet.

During the mixing process, no-one noticed a fine explosive powder had dusted some of the tiles in the room. On 9 October, as one of the filing cabinets was being slid across the tiles, it ignited the coating, which caused a loud bang. This drew the attention of neighbours, who were told it was either a balloon or a car tyre that had burst. In truth, the entire tonne of explosive mix had come within millimetres of detonating the suburb. Unfortunately, none of the neighbours reported their suspicions to the police.

Despite their near demise, the team continued their work, more carefully and no doubt more nervously. Eventually the assembly process was finished and the components were installed in the van. Inside the van, 1.125 tonnes of explosive powder sat neatly packed in 12 filing cabinets. A booster charge of 25 kilograms of pure TNT was attached to the block of filing cabinets. Woven between and around the block was 150 metres of PETN (Pentaerythritol tetranitrate) detonating cord. To ensure the most rapid explosive rate, 94 detonators, each containing 200 grams of highly explosive military grade RDX (Research Department Explosive), were connected. The cake was ready to be cooked.

JIMI'S CAKE

By 12 October everything was ready, including the two suicide bombers who were taken on a guided tour past Paddy's Pub and the Sari Club. On that tour the bombing sequence was outlined: the first suicide bomber (Iqbal) would explode a vest he was wearing inside Paddy's Pub, sending those that weren't killed by the bomb onto the street outside the Sari Club, where the second suicide bomber (Jimi) would be sitting in readiness with the 1-tonne bomb hidden inside the Mitsubishi van.[73] When surrounded by foreigners, Jimi would activate the truck bomb. Simultaneously, a motorcycle bomb would be remotely exploded (by phone) near the US consulate – so the Americans would know they were the focus of the attack.

During the day, the bombers were kept religiously and psychologically on course with Mukhlas's reinforcement that their martyrdom would provide a peaceful place with Allah for 70 members of their family. Additionally, the bombers themselves would be free of torment, never be hungry, and would receive a bounty including 72 large-breasted virgins who would attend to their every need.[74]

As the critical time approached, convinced of his rewards, Jimi wrote his last will and testament, which he used as a platform to encourage more Muslims to murder:

Today there is so much work that must be completed for
the sake of the struggle, and pray that my martyrdom will

DEFEATING TERROR

be the trigger for the growth of the *mujahedin* ... And today, I prove that I am a child of DI/NII [Indonesian Islamic State] who is ready to sacrifice his life for Islam. If you all truly want to build a return to the glory of the NII that today is buried, pour your blood out in order that you are not all ashamed before God ...

Jimi also wrote a note to his parents:

Mother pray for me so I will fight to defend Islam. I want Jihad to defend Islam which is crushed by non-believers. I only ask for prayers from mother, father so that in order that I die *Sahid* [martyr].[75]

Contrary to his irrational belief that there was a holy war being fought and that mass murder of innocent people was justified, Jimi also asked that his clothes be given to the poor.

*

That night, about 10.45 pm on 12 October 2002, Kosuke Suzuki, 34, and his new bride, Yuka, 33, both from Yokohama, had just finished dining at a restaurant near their hotel in Kuta. While this wasn't the first time they had been to Bali, it was their first time as a married couple. The pair had landed the

110

JIMI'S CAKE

day before on a Japanese Airlines flight as part of an organised tour. As honeymooners in Bali do, the pair would have been enjoying every minute, absorbing as much of each other and of the chaotic fun-filled Balinese atmosphere as they could.

After their meal, the couple flagged down a *bemo* (Balinese taxi) to take them into the centre of Kuta, a kilometre or so further along the one-way Legion Street. As their *bemo* merged into the traffic conga line, a white Mitsubishi L300 van appeared from a side street and slotted itself into the narrow gap in front. Inside the van were Imron, in the driver's seat, and beside him sat Jimi and Iqbal, who was wearing an explosive vest hidden under an oversized shirt.

A few minutes later the van stopped, blocking the traffic, as Imron got out of the driver's seat and was promptly picked up by Idris on a Yamaha motorcycle. Jimi, a learner driver, slid into the driver's seat. Moments later, the L300 lurched forward as Jimi applied too much accelerator and the van moved abruptly, suddenly allowing the bank of traffic to flow once again. The Japanese couple and the *bemo* driver probably didn't raise an eyebrow; it was chaotic, but that was nothing out of the ordinary for Legion Street on a Saturday night.

While Jimi and Iqbal were slowly but surely making their way to the destination, followed directly behind by the newlyweds' *bemo*, Idris parked the Yamaha F1ZR on a quiet street. Imron got off and dialled a phone number. Seconds

DEFEATING TERROR

later the motorcycle bomb exploded harmlessly near the US Consulate about 20 kilometres away. Then the pair headed off to the mosque, where they hid as Jimi and Iqbal made their way towards their ultimate destination.

Near the Sari Club, Jimi managed to momentarily stop the vehicle as Iqbal got out and walked into Paddy's Pub. Then Jimi deliberately stalled the vehicle outside the Sari Club, initiating a chorus of beeping horns. But the van wasn't going anywhere.

A crowd started to gather around the van. Jimi had locked the doors and sat there ignoring them. Suddenly there was a blast from inside Paddy's Pub, shattering windows along the opposite side of the street. Smoke started pluming from the pub as panicked people ran from the fiery hell to the sanctuary of the street – where Jimi was parked.

It's not known what conversation, if any, was had between the two honeymooners and the *bemo* driver, but the sight of blackened and bleeding Paddy's Pub patrons stumbling from inside the ruins must have caused them to panic. But it was already too late to escape their fate.

In the van, Jimi pushed the switch. Instantaneously, an apocalyptic blast burst from the vehicle, propelling the honeymooners' *bemo* high into the air. This was no Hollywood slow-motion scene where people had time to dive for cover. The battering-ram blast shredded flesh from bones, heads from bodies and sent red-hot razor-sharp steel shrapnel and

JIMI'S CAKE

glass into everyone and everything. Then came the fireball. Its intense heat instantly vaporised people in the immediate area, transforming fit young bodies into rag dolls and combusting shopfronts up and down Legion Street – leaving nothing in its wake but fire, panic, chaos and death.

Defenceless, innocent people, of all religious denominations, cultures and countries were killed. Jimi's cake was cooked; the cowards' work was done.

BIG FISH

Jimi's blast was recorded by seismic equipment at precisely 31 seconds past 11.03 pm and was felt over 20 kilometres from the site. The attacks killed 202 people from 21 countries and injured 168 others. The complexity of the attack and the fact that it involved Indonesia's first suicide bombers demonstrated a significant escalation in terrorist activities in Southeast Asia. It was indisputably an attack with global ramifications. As such, offers of medical, technological and intelligence support flooded in from around the world. Within days, a multinational investigation task force led by Indonesian police was established in Bali. Several countries committed police resources to assist in tracking down the culprits, including a significant contingent from the AFP.

Made Pastika, a devout Hindu, was nominated to head up the Bali investigation by Da'i Bachtiar (chief of the INP), a committed Muslim.[76] The multinational team supporting them was an amalgamation of Muslim, Christian, Hindu, Buddhist,

BIG FISH

Jewish, Shinto, atheist and agnostic men and women from the US, Britain, Australia, Sweden, Denmark, Greece, Japan, Germany, France, Holland and the Philippines. There was no religious bigotry in the minds of these officers. They were investigating a mass murder, not a religion, not a culture – simply a horrendous hate crime motivated by perverted religious beliefs.

With the assistance of Australian personnel and technology, the Indonesian police formed several advanced electronic field tracking teams that could pinpoint with a reasonable degree of accuracy the location of any 'active' mobile phone. These multinational and religiously diverse tracking teams worked cohesively and tirelessly as they hunted throughout Indonesia for the killers and their accomplices.

Complementing these efforts were international intelligence sources from participating countries. This information guided the Indonesian police to approach Abu Bakar Bashir in his home village of Solo on 19 October 2002. Bashir denied any involvement in the attacks, telling police that Islam is a religion of peace and that Jamaah Islamiyah is a myth that has been spread by the CIA and Western governments to victimise Muslims.

Bashir agreed to be interviewed by the police the following day, but later informed them he was suddenly suffering a respiratory and stomach complaint and was going to hospital. An arrest warrant alleging his involvement with the Christmas Eve

115

DEFEATING TERROR

2000 church bombing attacks was handed to Bashir's lawyers and from that point he remained under police guard in hospital.

When the news of his arrest spread, the hospital was attacked and a riot ensued between police and Muslim hardline supporters of Bashir. Under the constant barrage of attacks and threats to blow up the hospital, almost 300 Indonesian police were needed to extricate Bashir to Jakarta.

While this was occurring, in Bali the forensic examination of a piece of wreckage found on a roof near the Sari Club revealed the chassis number of the L300 van. Checks confirmed it was registered to Amrozi. Prior to the attack, Amrozi had ground off identification marks from the car; however, he had missed one. This mistake led to police raiding his home in Tenggulun, East Java, on 5 November 2002. Amrozi, who would become known as the 'smiling assassin' due to his constant oversized smirk, gave up peacefully and confessed to buying the explosives and to being involved in the attack. He also named the other JI members involved, including his two brothers, Mukhlas and Imron, who had fled days earlier.

This information led to several Islamic schools being raided by Indonesian police. Uncovered were terrorist planning documents, explosives, firearms and thousands of rounds of ammunition. Several JI members on the periphery of the Bali attack were arrested thanks to this evidence, including some who provided Samudra's current 'active' phone number.

BIG FISH

That number, together with the treasure trove of electronic evidence stored in Amrozi's phone, injected significant momentum to the very secretive tracking teams. One team was successful in isolating Samudra's phone to the Merak ferry terminal on the north-western tip of Java. Indonesian police then staked out the ferry terminal and arrested a disguised Samudra as he attempted to board a ferry to Sumatra on 21 November 2002. Just like Amrozi, Samudra didn't resist arrest and made a full confession naming others involved, including JI's leader, Hambali. On his computer police found Islamic propaganda, speeches by bin Laden, beheading videos and hundreds of pornographic images of Western women.

Unfortunately, shortly after Samudra's arrest, information about the advanced tracking technology that was used to locate him was leaked to the media. When the story broke in Australia and Indonesia, Mukhlas, Azhari, Imron, Idris and Dulmatin, who were each being covertly pursued by tracking teams, immediately disposed of their phones' SIM cards. This was a major blow to the investigation, as the terrorists started regularly changing their phone numbers by purchasing various prepaid SIM cards.

As there was no requirement to show identification documents when purchasing a new SIM card, and with about 2000 SIM cards being activated or deactivated each week throughout Indonesia, this tactic greatly reduced the effectiveness of the tracking teams – but it didn't dampen their resolve.[77]

Joint Tracking Team 3 was led by Herlan Susilo, a 41-year-old experienced Indonesian detective. Susilo was a devout Muslim and was no doubt disgusted that someone had used his religion as an excuse for mass murder. Under his leadership, Tracking Team 3 had been close to locating Mukhlas on several occasions. However, it seemed whenever they got to within a kilometre or two of his location, Mukhlas either turned his phone off, or he travelled into an area where there was no mobile phone reception. Adding to their frustration, they had been unable to re-establish a tracking signal since the media published the tracking technology story. They had been closing in on Mukhlas's phone signal, which was moving south from the city of Malang towards the small town of Kepanjen in East Java, when the signal suddenly stopped. For the next three days, the team waited covertly in the area in the hope that Mukhlas would turn his phone on.

On the morning of 4 December 2002, Susilo left his team in place and returned to Malang where another tracking team had arrested a suspect.[78] The suspect told police that he knew that Makmuri, a JI member from the Kepanjen area, had 'a big fish' staying at his house. That was all Susilo needed to hear. He and his team sped to Kepanjen and met with the Kepanjen district police chief.

BIG FISH

Subsequent police and witness accounts, including Mukhlas's own, was that at about 3 pm Susilo's team and some local police crept into the small suburb and secretly surrounded Makmuri's two-bedroom house.[79] The police chief, who had changed from his uniform into a T-shirt and jeans, and a similarly clad Susilo walked onto the small landing at the front of the house. The police chief knocked as Susilo drew his Smith and Wesson six-shot revolver from its well-used leather holster. Moments later, Makmuri's wife cracked open the door and looked out at the two men.

'Polisi!' Susilo yelled as he shouldered past the police chief and pushed the door open. Makmuri's wife reeled backwards, just maintaining her balance as the two police officers pushed past her.

'Polisi!' Susilo yelled again as he entered one of the bedrooms with his pistol leading the way.

With Susilo's eyes yet to adjust from the bright sunlight outside to the darkened bedroom, he was taken by surprise as Mukhlas's hand grabbed Susilo's firearm. Instinctively, Susilo clutched the revolver with both hands. As he did so, Mukhlas's free hand flew upward into Susilo's groin where it attached with a vice-like grip, buckling Susilo at the knees. Then the police chief entered the fracas with a solid right knee catching Mukhlas's rib cage, propelling him onto the floor. As Susilo re-holstered his firearm, the police chief dived on top of Mukhlas,

DEFEATING TERROR

who was crawling towards a black bum bag on the floor in the corner of the room.

Despite the weight of the hefty police chief, Mukhlas managed to reach the bag with one hand and pulled heavily on the zip, revealing a loaded US Army pistol. Susilo stamped on Mukhlas's hand, causing him to release his grip. As Susilo kicked the bag along the floor to the door, Mukhlas's legs went into overdrive, kicking free of the police chief. As Mukhlas stood up, Susilo grabbed him in a bear hug and pushed him against the wall. The police chief joined in and made it a three-man standing scrum. Just then, two uniformed officers arrived at the door.

One of the uniformed officers dived into the rotating mass of legs and grabbed what he thought was Mukhlas's leg, but was in fact his chief's leg. With great gusto, he lifted the leg, causing his boss to fall and the entire scrum to avalanche to the ground. The fall knocked the wind out of Mukhlas, giving Susilo an opportunity to wrestle a pair of handcuffs onto his skinny wrists. At that point Mukhlas capitulated. It had been a long and arduous hunt, but Susilo had finally landed the big fish.

In the weeks that followed Mukhlas's capture, the multinational police teams made several more arrests. Imron took extreme measures to evade capture. However, with 35 JI members arrested since the bombing, and most providing full confessions, it was only a matter of time until his name was

BIG FISH

added to the list of arrestees. On 14 January 2003, dressed in a women's burqa, Imron was arrested as he attempted to leave Indonesia.

Spectacularly missing from the arrest list were Hambali, Azhari, Dulmatin and Idris. The police knew each had played a crucial role in the Bali attack and now all four were at the top of the most wanted list.

In February 2003, disguised and using a false Malaysian passport, Azhari travelled to Thailand undetected and met with Hambali in a rented apartment in Satun Province in southern Thailand. Following the arrest of Mukhlas, Hambali had resumed leadership of JI. However, at this meeting it's likely he forewarned Azhari that he would need to take over the organisation's leadership if Hambali was subsequently arrested or killed. Relying on the authority of bin Laden's recent *fatwa* (urging attacks on the US and its allies) Hambali intended to use the human internet the *usroh* web provided to supervise the next attack: on the JW Marriott Hotel in Jakarta.[80] As his likely successor, he made Azhari the commander responsible for that operation.

Azhari must have returned to Jakarta with his head spinning with the thought that one day, possibly sooner rather than later, he might be responsible for all JI operations. Of more immediate concern was to successfully oversee the next JI attack, which was scheduled for within just six months.

From media reporting around the Bali One bombing, Azhari had learned police could electronically track mobile phones. He'd also learned this could be thwarted by using multiple SIM cards and leaving his phone turned off. What couldn't be managed as easily was the flow of critical information from arrested JI members to the police, which had led to so many rapid arrests after the Bali One bombing.

The solution was to compartmentalise information, so if one person was arrested they would have limited information that could lead to the arrest of others. Azhari would install this as a protocol for the JW Marriott bombing; his killing evolution continued.

THE UNNAMED

After returning to Indonesia, Azhari contacted his protege, Top, in Malaysia and asked him to recruit potential suicide bombers for the next attack. Top agreed and they arranged to meet in Sumatra.[81]

Hambali successfully arranged for $89,000 cash for the Marriott attack to be transported by his brother, Gungun Rusman Gunawan, from an Al-Qaeda operative in Pakistan to a JI messenger in Indonesia.[82] The *usroh* network then channelled the money to where it was required to purchase TNT, RDX, ammonium nitrate, potassium chlorate and other chemicals.

Regardless of how many arrests the police made, the human internet of the *usrohs* would simply adapt and find another information path. Unfortunately for them, this now also included some Indonesian police and intelligence agents. As such, a small number of tracking teams, analysts and intelligence assets based in Jakarta worked in a very secretive unit within the recently formed elite counterterrorism unit Detachment 88.[83]

There is some conjecture about the numbering of the Detachment. Some say it was named in honour of the 88 Australians killed in Bali One, others that it was an Indonesian mispronunciation of the detachment's primary sponsor, the US Anti-Terrorist Assistance (ATA) program, and some simply that 88 is a lucky Asian number. Regardless of its nomenclature, the elite Detachment 88 was funded by the US ($130 million) and Australia ($35 million) and was formed specifically for counterterrorism investigations. It has now been publicly reported that:

> With a river of cash for cutting edge equipment, a joint project between Australia, Indonesia and the United States would funnel money through the US Diplomatic Security Service to mould this new unit into what is, in effect, a Special Forces detachment. The CIA, FBI and even the US Secret Service work alongside the Australian Federal Police (AFP) and Australian Special Forces to run recruits through a gruelling training program at a secret compound on Megamendung, which lies 50 kms south of Jakarta.[84]

In the utmost secrecy, the technologically advanced elite unit was housed in a covert location away from the main Detachment 88 offices. The men and women working inside this unit were

THE UNNAMED

almost entirely isolated from their home organisations and the broader Detachment 88. The camaraderie, commitment and loyalty to each other galvanised the Indonesian and Australian counterparts into a very tight-knit, trusted team.

Knowledge of the unit's existence was a tightly held secret even within Detachment 88 itself and it never appeared on official organisational structures or planning documents. To avoid discovery, the unit remained unnamed. These measures were very effective in halting Detachment 88's most secret information from being leaked or sold to JI's extensive network.

Without the benefit of any leaked information, Azhari remained very much on the run as he prepared for the Marriott bombing. Constantly on the move, he stayed at various locations under false names and only for short periods of time. In April 2003, Azhari met with Top in Medan, North Sumatra, and the pair travelled by public transport to Bengkulu, South Sumatra. There they met a group of former Al-Mukmin Islamic school students at the home of Asmar Latin Sani, a 28-year-old committed Islamic militant.[85] Sani was a member of an affiliated Islamic group (Laskar Khos) but swore the JI oath and gave an undertaking to be the next suicide bomber.

Having learned from JI's past failings, Azhari implemented the strict compartmentalisation of information so most who assisted with preparations for the attack weren't told the precise target, including Idris and Sani himself.

Despite the assistance of Hambali's cash, the group were soon running short of funds. With the core group all working full-time on bomb preparations, there was no income to pay for rental accommodation, travel, equipment purchases and additional explosives. Azhari charged Idris with forming his own independent team, focused on getting more funds.

Azhari's compartmentalisation paid dividends a few days later when Idris, assisted by 10 other JI operatives, burst into the Lippo Bank in the centre of Medan with guns blazing. Three bank employees were killed and several others were injured. Idris and his group escaped with $20,000, but were rounded up within days. Idris was arrested on 12 June 2003 and made a full confession to assisting with the Bali attacks. Without being able to elaborate further, he also told police that there would be another big attack soon, maybe in Jakarta.

The arrests had prevented the loot from getting to Azhari's group in Bengkulu. Fortunately for Azhari, Al-Qaeda had just sent a sum of $100,000 cash to Hambali as a 'congratulations for the Bali attack' and to 'encourage more Jihad'.[86] Hambali was subsequently able to send a payment through the *usroh* to the group.

Now adequately financed, the group purchased explosives and arranged for them to be delivered to several addresses in Bengkulu. Then Azhari, assisted by Top, Dulmatin and previous Islamic school students Tohir and Ismail, mixed the

THE UNNAMED

chemicals, tested electronic circuit boards and pre-assembled the bomb into modular parts that could easily and quickly be reassembled.

The next month, July 2003, Azhari and Top caught a Lion Air flight to Jakarta to conduct reconnaissance and preparation for the Marriott attack. Sitting next to them was a Muslim mother of two, Ramlah. On the flight, she noticed Azhari and Top appeared to be talking secretively in hushed Malaysian accents, so she listened intently to them. While their conversation was guarded, it was suspicious enough for Ramlah to take note of their appearance and report what she knew to police when she arrived in Jakarta. The unnamed unit within Detachment 88 received the information and, for a number of hours, were able to track a phone number associated with the purchase of the tickets through the busy streets of Jakarta – until once again the signal stopped.

This was particularly unfortunate as Top and Azhari were en route to a housing complex where final preparations for the Marriott bombing would be completed. The ramshackle rented house at Kemuning Raya 26, in the poor suburb of East Pejaten, South Jakarta, had most of the windows boarded up and those that weren't had three-year-old newspapers taped across the inside of the glass. It was one of the houses JI had used as a storage location when preparing for the Christmas Eve bombings in 2000. As the house had not been raided by the

DEFEATING TERROR

police in the aftermath, it was clearly not on the police radar, making it a perfect safe house to once again launch an attack.

At that address Azhari, Dulmatin, Sani, Tohir and Ismail assembled and installed the Azhari-designed plug-and-play modular explosive packages, weighing over 150 kilograms, into the back of a Toyota Kijang van.

On 5 August 2003, around noon, Sani was in the passenger's seat of the Kijang van as Azhari drove towards the Marriott. He pulled into a parking spot on the busy main road, then activated the bomb's timing circuit and got out of the van. The plan was for Sani to drive the van as close to the foyer as possible and then detonate the bomb. Regardless, Azhari had set the 20-minute timing circuit on its countdown. Irrespective of Sani having a change of heart, or the police intervening, the bomb was going to explode. Now, not even Azhari could stop the inevitable explosion.

As instructed, Sani drove steadily further along the road and then carefully turned into the Marriott's circular driveway. As he slowly approached the building, he must have noticed there only seemed to be Indonesians waiting at the entrance; none of the white people that Azhari had told him to look for. He pulled into the taxi zone at the front, perhaps to reconsider what he should do next. Azhari watched as a security guard approached the van. Most likely frustrated that Sani hadn't driven to the very entrance of the Marriott and self-detonated,

THE UNNAMED

Azhari pressed the preset number in his phone. Seconds later, his creation released its cataclysmic force.

Sani was instantly decapitated by the blast. His head smashed its way through a fifth-floor window, where it would later be found by police. The 33-storey American-owned building became a bombsite of devastation and death.

Close by, Azhari must have been like an excited child. Remaining for a few minutes not far from the scene, he would have heard the sirens and screams echo up and down the street and watched as office papers fluttered in the whirlwind created by the blast.

His elation would have been mixed with some concern; he knew the phone call he made was a tasty platter of forensic evidence for the police. From the first Bali bombing confessions, they knew Azhari mixed the Bali bombs and his call would soon prove the Marriott bomb also came from his lethal menu of explosive recipes.

It was Azhari's signature dish.

UNLEASHED

Minutes after enjoying the Marriott explosion, Azhari was picked up on a motor scooter by Top and they fled the area before the inevitable roadblocks could be established. This was their preferred method of transport because they could wear helmets with dark visors, completely concealing their identity. It's not uncommon in Indonesia for motorcycle riders to wear their helmets when stopping at places such as shops, markets or when purchasing fuel, so their tactic didn't raise suspicion.

Azhari and Top motored their way to a boarding house at 24A Kembang, in the city of Bandung. The ferocity of the Marriott bomb that day would have only been matched by Azhari's rage when he and Top listened to the BBC radio news in the boarding house that night. The news reported that only one of the 12 people killed in the attack was a foreigner, a Dutchman; the rest were Indonesian Muslims. Nearly all of the 150 wounded people were also Indonesians. The attack had been a spectacular failure.

UNLEASHED

While Azhari was silently brooding in the boarding house, Tohir and Ismail, who had travelled east from Jakarta prior to the bombing, arrived at an apartment in Cirebon. Neither had heeded Azhari's instructions to destroy their SIM cards. It appears both men assumed Azhari was paranoid and had underestimated the technical ability and tenacity of the tracking teams. Days later both men were arrested and subsequently made full confessions, including the likely whereabouts of Azhari and Top. Chillingly, both men told police that Azhari had started wearing a bomb in a bum bag which he carried with him at all times, ready to detonate if the police approached him.

Detachment 88 kept the arrests secret from the media, allowing them some time to conduct covert intelligence checks with Bandung boarding houses and known JI associates in the area. During this period, either Hambali contacted Azhari or vice versa. Either way, it was missed by the Indonesian–Australian tracking teams, but was picked up in Thailand, most likely by a Thai police–CIA tracking team.

Hambali had gone to extraordinary lengths to avoid detection, including having plastic surgery to his face. But it wasn't enough to save him on this occasion. After locating him, the Thai tracking team covertly observed and recorded him for a number of days to learn as much as they could about one of the world's most wanted terrorists, his methodologies and his contacts. On 11 August 2003 (six days after the Marriott bombing), Thai police raided Hambali's flat in Ayutthaya, about 70 kilometres outside Bangkok. There, he and his Malaysian wife were arrested without incident.[87]

The capture of Hambali made headlines around the world. Following his arrest, he was taken to CIA black sites and eventually Guantanamo Bay for interrogation in respect to his involvement with multiple bombing attacks. These included the bombing of the USS *Cole*, 9/11, the Bali night clubs, the Marriott hotel, the Christmas Eve church attacks and the aborted Singapore attack plan. It had been a very busy three years for Hambali.

The news confirming Hambali's arrest would have come as a shock to Top, but more so Azhari. At that point, he learned that he'd just inherited the role of JI's operational commander, responsible for thousands of radicalised JI members.

This change in leadership was to bring about a very dangerous transition in JI's attack philosophy. Terrorist organisations are, by their nature, filled with radical fanatics. Within that context, some are the extreme within the extreme. When one of these people assumes the leadership, as often happens, any skerrick of morality, restraint and conscience is extinguished. Azhari's reign would do just that.

JI had always sought religious approval from their spiritual advisors, such as Sungkar and Bashir, before targeting places and killing people. Without such an approval, an attack could not

UNLEASHED

be legitimised under Islam. Within the terrorist environment, this is the last point where some level of restraint can intervene. Moderate Muslim clerics who have peace and humanity at heart would dissuade such attacks, so of course only known radical clerics are consulted. While it appears there is no shortage of demagogue clerics prepared to give their religious imprimatur for mass killings, some will add a thin veneer of decency by insisting that Muslim deaths should be minimised – a small mercy in the scheme of mass killing events, but a tiny thread of humanity nonetheless.

For those who are vulnerable or susceptible to radicalisation, or those who need a 'moral' excuse to kill in the name of Islam, religious approval can be used as a lever of influence, paving the way to a clear conscience and a sense of righteousness. For this reason JI had, until that point, always previously sought and gained religious approval.

It seems Azhari wasn't prepared to risk any restraint or intervention in his plans, even by approaching well-known radical Islamic leaders such as Bashir, who would likely rubber-stamp any request. Azhari disposed of the requirement for religious approval for attacks based on the preaching of Abu Qatada al-Filistini, a perverted Palestinian–Jordanian Muslim scholar who specialised in the subject of violent Jihad.

In his teachings, al-Filistini preached that in cases where an attack is required in defence of Islam (*jihad difai*), there is no requirement for any spiritual or organisational approval. Furthermore, it is an obligation for all Muslims to attack independently (*fard al ain*).[88] Al-Filistini promoted lone-wolf type attacks and encouraged they be undertaken wherever it was even 'perceived' that Islam was under attack (*jihad fardiyah*).

After arriving in London from Jordan, al-Filistini taught at the Four Feathers Community Centre near Regent's Park, which became a hub for radical Islamic teaching.[89] This centre was less than one hour's drive from where Azhari was attending university in Reading at the time. It's entirely possible that Azhari met or at least listened to the preaching of al-Filistini when he was completing his doctorate in the 1990s and this may explain his deviation from the religious sanctioning that JI previously adhered to.

Relying on al-Filistini's philosophy, Azhari no longer required any external frame of reference for religious guidance. Morally, legally and religiously he now had a legitimate excuse and an open invitation to murder anyone he considered to be in any way connected to an attack on Islam. In his mind this would have also included Muslims who believed in democracy and Indonesian law; there was only one law, Sharia law, and if you didn't live by it your penalty was death. Hypocritically, Azhari used his religion as a justification for killing, but didn't adhere to any of its urgings for restraint, compassion or goodwill.

UNLEASHED

After the death of Sungkar in late 1999, JI became more aggressive and less controlled under the lacklustre stewardship of Bashir. The organisation had conducted several attacks and killed not only Westerners, but many Muslims. This had eroded some of the silent community support that JI had enjoyed for several years in Indonesia. If the authorities and rational Muslims were concerned with JI's recent activities, this new concept would shock even those with the most steadfast Islamic views. And now that Azhari was entirely unleashed, his first target was Australia.

In late November in a boarding house in Bandung, Azhari and Top commenced planning and preparations to bomb the Australian embassy in Jakarta. Under recently introduced Indonesian terrorism laws, boarding houses were required to report the names of any guests staying for longer than 24 hours to the local police. As such, the owner of the Bandung boarding house had duly reported the names and addresses that Azhari and Top had provided when they presented their false identification to him on arrival.

On 29 October 2003 Bayu, a young Muslim man, was working at the boarding house when he was approached by Rafi, the Muslim team leader of a tracking team that had been hunting Azhari for weeks on end.[90] Typically, members of these tracking teams, including their Australian counterparts, looked more like vagrants than police, particularly after living it rough

DEFEATING TERROR

in Azhari's wake for several weeks. Considering his vagabond appearance, it would have been a surprise to Bayu when Rafi produced his small gold Polisi badge and asked about the new boarders.

Rafi was told that the two men were quiet and largely kept to themselves, usually venturing out at night time or early morning. It may have been when Bayu mentioned the men had Malaysian accents, or that he thought they were engineering students because they had carried electronic component boxes and rolls of wire into the room, that Rafi realised he was in very close proximity to his volatile quarry.

Rafi relayed his suspicion that the boarders were Azhari and Top to Bayu and requested he keep their conversation strictly confidential, then departed. As a seasoned covert operative, Rafi would have left with a deliberately slow gait and nonchalant demeanour, disguising his elevated levels of excitement and adrenaline.

Rafi's tracking team was too small to effectively surround the boarding house, particularly considering the violent nature of the two people they were intending to arrest. As time was of the essence, Rafi left his team in place to observe the boarding house and he contacted the local police commander, seeking additional police to support the imminent raid.

While Rafi was arranging reinforcements, Bayu, who had no previous criminal history, appears to have found himself morally flummoxed. As a law-abiding Indonesian citizen, he would naturally side with the police. The conundrum was created by the fact he didn't have two 'normal' criminals staying in the lodgings; they were Muslim men on a Jihad. This changed everything. On one hand, he had a Muslim police officer seeking his assistance with the arrest of two indiscriminate murderers and, on the other, a religious obligation to assist those on a Jihad.

It was a conflicting case of legal pluralism bringing Indonesian law into stark conflict with Sharia law. Indonesian citizens and their court system had been struggling with this juxtaposition since the country's constitution enshrined their national legal principles in 1945.[91]

Presumably after a period of thought, and certainly before the police arrived in force, Bayu sided with Sharia law and tipped off Azhari and Top. Almost immediately, the pair burst from their room and ran in different directions, surprising the police. Top eluded his pursuers in short order. However, Azhari, who was wearing a heavy backpack, had Rafi and others in close pursuit. Unencumbered, they were rapidly making ground on him. Realising his predicament, Azhari exited through a laneway and ran into the local marketplace that was crammed with hundreds of people shopping at stalls erected under a multicoloured patchwork of polyester tarps. There, Azhari was surrounded by armed police with their weapons held high,

DEFEATING TERROR

scattering the crowd in the immediate vicinity. According to one report, Rafi threatened to shoot Azhari in the head if he didn't surrender; a brave threat of accuracy, considering his nervously shaking wrist and the short barrel of his .38 revolver. It was then that Azhari played his trump card. He unzipped his bum bag and threatened to detonate a bomb.

This created a Mexican standoff that threatened the lives of the surrounding police and the crowd of rapidly gathering spectators. Siding with caution and humanity, eventually the police capitulated and allowed Azhari to flee.

Losing that confrontation must have been immensely frustrating for Rafi and his team. The remedy would have been to have a team of snipers surrounding Azhari.

That day would come. But not yet …

SHARIA LAW & HOLY WAR

Over the next three days, LABFOR (Indonesian police forensics) photographed, fingerprinted and took DNA samples from the partially completed bombs, chemicals and circuit diagrams from Azhari and Top's room. It was a treasure trove of forensic intelligence, primarily because Rafi's team had witnessed Azhari and Top leaving the room. For the first time LABFOR were able to collect samples that could be directly attributed to the Malaysian terror duo. Until that time there were no reliable police records of either man's fingerprints. Now they had two confirmed sets. These prints could be compared to all previous bomb scenes to confirm which attacks either Azhari, Top, or both were involved with.

LABFOR also took samples of the various powders and, with the assistance of the AFP, these were analysed and tested with the electronic circuit boards that had been left behind.

DEFEATING TERROR

Based on the quantity of bomb-making material left in the room, it was estimated that Azhari and Top were intending to make 10 body-pack suicide bombs. The construction of the circuit boards, type of 9-volt battery used and the unique potassium chlorate mixture were almost identical to those in the suicide vest and the motorcycle bomb used in the Bali One attack. This established the first confirmed forensic link between Azhari and that bombing. Subsequent testing and analysis inextricably linked Azhari to the Marriott and Christmas Eve bombing attacks. He was now Indonesia's most wanted terrorist.

Unaware of his new title, Azhari met up with Top at a prearranged location days later and stayed with a JI member.[92] Both had by then not just thrown their SIM cards away, but had ditched their phones completely. This may have been because they assessed it was the phone handset that had betrayed their location at the boarding house. They had up until that time been communicating with key JI members by turning their phones on momentarily, sending a coded text message and turning it off immediately, so the tracking teams couldn't locate them. This had been an effective tactic. However, after the close shave at the boarding house, it seems a combination of paranoia and an overestimation of law enforcement's ability to electronically track phones that were turned off convinced them that carrying phones at all left them susceptible.

140

SHARIA LAW & HOLY WAR

Without phones, now the men had to rely fully on JI's human internet and a supportive network of sympathetic Muslims to communicate. Via these means, Azhari had contacted Rois, aka Iwan Darmawan. Rois was a member of the ailing Darul Islam group, a fractured fanatical Islamic movement. Rois was a good-looking and charismatic young man who was able to gain the confidence of almost anyone from the outset. His short, meticulously maintained dark hair was stylishly brushed back. He wore modern thin-rimmed glasses that rested on a well-proportioned nose above his infectious smile and handsome chin. He looked like a friendly, confident and well-groomed young man. However his outwardly tolerant and friendly demeanour masked his inner hatred of non-Muslims, and those he described as 'weak' Muslims – those who weren't committed to or supportive of Sharia law. Rois's polished veneer allowed him to befriend people and to quickly gain their trust; he was a natural networker.

As soon as someone in Rois's wide network of acquaintances became disillusioned, depressed or fell on hard times, he would pounce, slowly and methodically manipulating their thoughts towards blaming their woes on the scourge of the West and the influence of non-believers 'invading' Indonesia. As part of his recruitment strategy he would offer them some financial assistance and direct their spiritual guidance to the radical teachings of Bashir. Most often this was a successful strategy that converted otherwise reasonable and fair-thinking Muslims to radical Islam and its fascist hatred and intolerance.

For JI, this was a good achievement, but it wasn't Rois's ultimate goal – he wanted them to give more. Rois would remain in contact with the most radical converts and systematically amplify their hate and convince them of the absolute need for Sharia law and holy war. He'd convince them, too, that they should give more. Rois's primary role in JI was to recruit suicide bombers – and he was a master at it.[93]

Azhari's paranoia of electronic and human surveillance was working overtime by June 2004, when he held a critical planning meeting with Rois, Top and a small number of others. Adding to this was his distrust of others within JI, who he suspected were assisting the police. His suspicion was fed by the continuous arrests of those close to him. In another unprecedented move to further compartmentalise information about his activities, he formed a new very small group called *Thoifah Muqatilah* (Arabic for 'Combat Unit').

Under Azhari's instruction, the *Thoifah Muqatilah* group were to operate in complete isolation from the rest of JI, use suicide bombing as their predominant attack technique, remain committed to martyrdom and adopt al-Filistini's approach to Jihad, which unshackled them from any clerical oversight. Apart from Top, other attendees were not told of the plan to bomb the Australian embassy – simply that an attack was being

SHARIA LAW & HOLY WAR

planned. To assist, Rois was tasked with recruiting suicide bombers, who were referred to as 'brides'. Either at that meeting or shortly thereafter, Rois nominated Heri Golun as a suitable bride for the next wedding, wherever that may be.

In August 2004, Azhari again assembled his group and informed those present that their next target would be the Australian embassy in Jakarta.[94] Apart from Azhari's hatred for Australia, justification for selecting that particular target was easily found in the recent success of Al-Qaeda. That group had exploded 10 bombs on four trains in Madrid earlier that year (March 2004), three days before Spain's national elections. The bombs killed 200 people and caused a voting backlash, resulting in a change of government. The attacks were effective in that they drained Spanish courage to the point where their troops were almost immediately withdrawn from Iraq. An inspiring and encouraging result for any would-be terrorists and, seemingly, proof positive that terror tactics work.

JI had been relentlessly hunted by INP teams closely supported by the AFP. With Australia's national elections mooted to be held later that year (October 2004), Azhari reasoned that a well-timed and effective attack on Australia's heart in Indonesia could result in a change of government and cause the withdrawal of the AFP from Indonesia and Australian troops from Iraq. Considering the success of Al-Qaeda over the Spanish, this would have been seen as a probable outcome if their attack was heinous enough; Australian deaths were critical to the objectives of their attack.

9 September 2004

About 10.15 am on the day of the attack, Nanda Daniel, a 24-year-old Indonesian university student, was sitting on a crowded bus travelling towards the Jakarta business hub of Kuningan. While the bus slowly made progress through the almost gridlocked traffic, Nanda focused on reading her book to pass the time.

Several kilometres away, in a rented house in Cikande Complex, Rois and Top were packing up all their belongings into boxes, duffel bags and backpacks. They would have been flooded with excitement and anticipation as they hurriedly loaded the goods into a small van at the front of the house.

Near the centre of Kuningan, Azhari was driving a similar van, but with a very different cargo. In the back of this innocent-looking white Daihatsu Zebra was almost one tonne of Azhari's specially designed explosive cocktail: 500 kilograms of potassium chlorate, 200 kilograms of sulphur compound and six boxes of TNT. As was his modus operandi, Azhari had expertly mixed and filled three plastic filing cabinets with the deadly chemical compound. The filing cabinets were laced together with detonator cord and wired to explode manually from inside the car, remotely from a mobile phone and also by means of a timed circuit.

SHARIA LAW & HOLY WAR

In the passenger's seat next to Azhari was the bride, Golun, who had purchased the van especially for his wedding, just three weeks earlier.[95] Since then, Golun had been taking driving lessons, courtesy of his recruiter, Rois. Now Golun could drive – just, but not well enough for Azhari to trust that he could make it through the confused traffic to the Australian embassy. To ensure Golun was within range of the Australian target, Azhari pulled over to the side of the busy roadway, just 400 metres from the embassy. The pair had been there the day before completing a reconnaissance run, so Golun knew precisely where to drive the deathly cargo. This time, Azhari was leaving nothing to chance in his hunt for Australian lives.

Wanting to look inconspicuous, Azhari walked into a small convenience store and watched as the Daihatsu jerked and bunny-hopped its way into the line of traffic. About 400 metres away, near the entry to the Australian embassy grounds, Nanda Daniel's bus heaved to a stop and Nanda and the other passengers began to shuffle their way along the aisle and out of the vehicle. As Nanda was about to step down from the bus, Golun erratically swung the Daihatsu van into the 'no parking' space at the entry to the embassy, where he stalled the vehicle.

A security officer immediately started walking towards the van, but was met midway by a ferocious force of heat and debris from the exploding Daihatsu. The blast caught Nanda as she was stepping from the bus, severely burning her and piercing

DEFEATING TERROR

her right hand with a piece of razor shrapnel that shattered one of her metacarpal bones.

The owners of the convenience store that Azhari was using as a lookout would later report they heard him scream, '*Allahu Akbar!*' as his hellfire blast shattered lives and shop windows up and down the street.

Despite being permanently scarred, both physically and mentally, Nanda was one of the lucky ones that day. But in the microseconds of that blast, 10 others were slain and 180 innocents were injured.

THE WEDDING PLANNERS

Immediately after the embassy bombing, Azhari and Top headed for a safe house that was provided by Irun Hidayat. At the time, Hidayat was 32 years old and had become a well-known and powerful Muslim cleric. He had joined the Darul Islam education system in 1987, where he became good friends with Rois and Imam Samudra. In 1999, he became head of the religious council of the Indonesian Muslim Workers Union in West Java. From that position of spiritual and industrial power, he appointed radical Muslims into high-value jobs within industries and companies that would support the goals of Darul Islam and JI – such is the reach of organised terrorism.

By late afternoon when Azhari and Top arrived at the safe house, Azhari's prewritten message had been released on the internet:

DEFEATING TERROR

> We decided to settle accounts with Australia, one of the worst enemies of God and Islam ... and a mujahideen brother succeeded in carrying out a martyr operation with a car bomb against the Australian embassy. It is the first of a series of attacks ... We advise Australians in Indonesia to leave this country or else we will transform it into a cemetery for them ... We advise the Australian government to withdraw its troops from Iraq. If our demand is not satisfied, we will deal them many painful blows. The lines of booby-trapped cars will have no end.
>
> Jemaah Islamiah [*sic*] in eastern Asia. [96]

Often terrorist groups, including Daesh (ISIS), Al-Qaeda and JI, attempt to wash away the guilt of collaterally killing other Muslims by surmising that bystanders who are pure and devoted Muslims are guaranteed a place in paradise because they were killed as part of a Jihad. On the other hand, if they were not and they had cooperated with infidels, then they deserved to die anyway.[97] Even for those who accepted this unhinged perspective, when it was made public that the Australian embassy attack had failed to kill any Australians, but had successfully slain 10 Indonesians, it must have been a bitter pill to swallow.

Despite his best efforts and worst intentions, Azhari had once again led a catastrophic failure. His mood likely deteriorated

THE WEDDING PLANNERS

over the next few days as media articles reported that both Australian and Indonesian leaders had condemned the attacks and, in response, the Indonesian government had invited more AFP to Indonesia to assist with the investigation – the opposite of the outcome he had been hoping for. Worse still, rather than inspiring other Muslims to rise up and fight, the attack had been a public relations nightmare for JI, with wide condemnation of the attack by most of the Muslim community.

The Indonesian–Australian investigation quickly identified the owner of the Daihatsu was Golun, whose identity was confirmed through DNA analysis as also being the suicide bomber. The rented house at the Cikande Complex and other safe houses used by the group in the lead-up to the attack were rapidly raided by police. With the assistance of the AFP, LABFOR forensically matched the chemical and DNA samples taken from the safe houses to both the Australian embassy bombsite and the Bandung boarding house – confirming Azhari and Top were involved in the latest attack. In response, Indonesian police offered a 2 billion rupiah reward (more than $100,000), for information that would lead to the arrest of either man. At a time when Indonesia's average annual salary was just $1150, this above everything else demonstrated the Indonesian government's ardent intention to capture the Malaysians.[98]

On 5 November 2004, Indonesian police arrested Rois and three other JI operatives in a house in Bogor, 25 kilometres outside Jakarta.[99] Rois made a full confession and provided valuable intelligence about the attack, JI's existing network and the possible whereabouts of Azhari and Top.

The relentless pursuit by Indonesian police and the AFP over the previous two years had, at this stage, resulted in more than 50 arrests. This provided the tracking teams with increasingly accurate intelligence on JI. While the organisation still had an estimated network of over 1500 members throughout Indonesia, it was becoming fragmented as a result of infighting and suspicion that some members within its own ranks had become police informants – and they had.

The pressure from law enforcement was also taking its toll on individual members, forcing some to leave the organisation. While JI as a whole had a reduced criminal capacity as members were less inclined to commit crimes for fear of being arrested, and some members wanted a hiatus from the attack campaign, Azhari's determination to continue his murderous path remained resolute.

When news of Rois's arrest was made public, Azhari informed Top to secretly prepare to flee the safe house without informing Hidayat, who they suspected would make a confession if arrested, just as Rois had. Covertly they divvied up a wad of $10,000 cash. The money had previously been shown to Golun, and promised it would be given to his family subsequent to his martyrdom. However, as is most often the

THE WEDDING PLANNERS

case with terrorist organisations, after a successful suicide attack the martyr's family receive little or nothing of what was promised. Perhaps there is honour among thieves, but patently not among terrorists.

Before dawn and prior to Hidayat waking, the two men crept from the house and would have then quietly pushed their motor scooter beyond Hidayat's hearing before starting its rattling two-stroke engine. Then they would have donned their dark-visored helmets and ridden away incognito.

Unfortunately, the trail goes cold on where the Malaysian pair were destined. However, the following day (17 September 2004), police smashed their way into Hidayat's safe house and arrested him. Hidayat immediately cooperated with the police and told them in detail about the planning, preparation and execution of the Australian embassy bombing. His information corroborated the account given by Rois and the others arrested with him, adding vital intelligence to the ever-closing police dragnet. However, Hidayat was unable to provide any details on the possible whereabouts of the deadly duo, but he did warn the police that nothing short of their deaths would stop their attacks – an accurate prediction.

With the police now seemingly less than 24 hours behind them, it's likely the Malaysians split in different directions, moving from boarding house to boarding house. As they'd done before, they would have continuously used false names and deliberately given false information on their next destination, to throw any subsequent police enquiries off their real track. It appears that during this period, the pair also avoided JI members who might succumb to the substantial reward money or later confess information to the police if arrested.

For Azhari to continue his Jihad, he needed to be able to communicate with Top. However, by this stage neither man was prepared to carry or use a mobile phone or to use the *usroh* network. Ingeniously, they established a new method of communication. Before separating, they created several false email accounts that they both had the passwords for. The purpose of this was to communicate with each other by writing an email and then saving it into the 'draft' folder, thereby avoiding sending the information via email, where it could be intercepted by the police.

The men knew that with a population of over 240 million Indonesians, there would be thousands of new email accounts created every week, making it virtually impossible for the police to single out their particular random-named accounts. The men planned to use different internet cafes to check if there was a new message in one of the draft folders and also to never use the same internet cafe twice. Azhari had created an electronic Fort Knox around his covert communications.[100]

For security, the men splintered from the original *Thoifah Muqatilah* group and formed another independent *Thoifah*

THE WEDDING PLANNERS

Muqatilah. For the next attack they agreed that Top, the more charismatic of the two, would recruit a small number of radicalised youths for use as the next brides while Azhari would build the cakes for the next wedding. To ensure the *Thoifah Muqatilah* would continue the attack campaign in the event of their deaths or incarceration, both men nominated their successor. Just as Hambali had done with Azhari, Azhari nominated Muhammad Cholili to be his replacement and Top similarly nominated a person still only known as 'Teddy', a young aspiring Jihadist.[101]

During the following eight weeks, there's no reliable record as to the location or activities of each man. Consistent with his personality, it's likely that Azhari continued to obsessively think how to improve his killing effectiveness, considering the humiliation of not killing any Australians in the embassy attack.

After a two-month blackout, Azhari visited an internet cafe where he cut and pasted a message from a thumb drive into an email which he saved into the draft folder for Top to access from wherever he was hiding. The loosely coded message said:

> Brother I have decided we should hold the next wedding
> in B [Bali]. Why? Because it will have a global impact. It
> is known around the world, better than Indonesia itself.
> A wedding there will be covered by the international

media. Our guests are foreign tourists from America and its allies, particularly businessmen – this will have more impact than inviting [killing] young people. To do this we need to change our tactics. Security is tighter, the police chief has increased the number of rats [police] to 256 from just 70. This makes it too risky to bring a big wedding cake [truck bomb] like last time. We will use a number of premade small cakes [backpacks] so the brides can walk easily to their weddings. We need four brides.[102]

Days later, Top went to an internet cafe with Teddy and accessed the draft folder of the email account, read the message and deleted it; that way Azhari would know that he had read the message.

A few weeks later, Top and Teddy arrived at the small blue-and-white concrete villa that Azhari had rented with Cholili in Batu, Malang (East Java).[103] Living with Azhari and Cholili in the villa was Arman, Azhari's latest recruit. Azhari, possibly with the assistance of others unidentified, had triggered the Islamic kill-switch inside Arman's head and lured him away from his farming life with the promise of $10,000 cash for his family if he were to martyr himself (*Sahid*). Like all radicalised Islamic people, Arman would have believed that dying *Sahid* would bring financial prosperity to his family in this life and assure them a place with him in paradise in the next. Additionally, he would have believed the many sins he had committed during his life would be immediately expunged upon his death and he would spend an eternity in utopia. Considering his poor family situation and his traditional Islamic background, the opportunity to achieve his highest purpose (martyrdom) and to demonstrate his religious commitment for the benefit of his family, it was probably a relatively easy decision for Arman to make.

The terrorists' villa was in a terrace of charming villas that lined a quiet road in the mountainous township. The iron fence at the front was painted blue and white to match the main building, which gave it a quaint street appeal. The only differentiating feature of their villa was that its windows were obscured by pages of newspaper that had been carefully taped on the inside of each window. Consequently, as Top and Teddy entered the compact three-bedroom house they were surprised at how dark it was, with just a single low-wattage bulb providing barely enough illumination for the compact living room. The thick rendered brick walls had at one stage been painted white, but age and use had dulled them to a dirty beige. The majority of the floor was raw concrete with some sections covered with white, mostly cracked, tiles.

Something that would have struck the newcomer, Teddy, as he and Top entered the well-sealed house, was the dank atmosphere that had manifested in the absence of sunlight and of the fresh cool mountain breezes that gently swirl their way

DEFEATING TERROR

up the side of the mountain ridge through Batu. Inside, the house smelled of stagnant humidity, spicy noodles, body odour and the penetrating acidic fumes of smouldering hot soldering irons – the scent of a bomb factory. While it may have been foreign to Teddy, it would have been the familiar smell of excitement and productivity to Azhari and Top.

By this stage, Top had developed the ability to manipulate the vulnerable and steer religiously wayward youth onto the path of violent Jihad – a skill he had used with great effect after viewing Azhari's email. By the time he met with Azhari, Cholili and Arman in the villa, Top had already successfully recruited one bride and was in the process of radicalising others.[104]

When Top and Teddy arrived, Azhari spelled out in detail his desire to go back and bomb Bali a second time. His plan was to send four suicide bombers to Bali as soon as possible to undertake their own personal reconnaissance and report their findings directly to him. Azhari particularly wanted them to catalogue what most tourists were wearing, what types of backpacks they used, what shoes they wore and the most popular places and times where tourists gathered.

Azhari was so concerned about failing yet again to kill Australians, he decided to be extremely thorough. He precisely planned and recorded all the information in detail, including a precis of conversations with the brides-to-be, on his laptop.

THE WEDDING PLANNERS

Over the next few weeks he would write what would subsequently become known as 'The Bali Project' document, a 34-page intricately detailed plan for the Bali Two attack, timed to the second.[105] It was later recovered by police and it opened a window into Azhari's dark mind and revealed the callous activities of the group leading up to the bombing.

After the meeting, Top and Teddy returned to their hideout in Semarang, an eight-hour drive west of Malang. There, Top completed his JI talent-spotting and recruited another three willing bombers whom he promptly sent to Bali. Over the next few weeks Azhari, assisted by Arman and Cholili, completed assembling over 20 modular bombs in various shapes and sizes so they could be concealed in a variety of different objects.

In early September 2005, Top contacted Azhari and advised that the recruits had returned from their Bali reconnaissance journey. The go-betweens, Cholili and Teddy, met in Surabaya near the bus terminal. There for the first time Cholili met the four brides he would take to meet Azhari. They were Misno, a 30-year-old chicken farmer; Ayip Hidayat, 23 years old and unemployed; Salik Firdaus, a 30-year-old religious teacher; and Anif Solchanudin, a 24-year-old mobile phone salesman.[106] All six men were the poisonous products of the radical Islamic school system. In fact, Salik and Misno had become close friends at the same radical institution, the Sayahadah Islamic boarding school (near Ngruki), where they were psychologically branded for life

157

DEFEATING TERROR

with the virtues of suicide killing. The childhood friends were now just a matter of weeks away from sharing their ultimate scholastic goal together.

Cholili drove the four brides back to Azhari's bomb-factory villa in Batu. There Azhari sat with his laptop at the ready and interviewed the men. He asked a series of questions about their reconnaissance and typed a detailed account of their findings into his bombing master plan.

At first it was suggested that nightclubs would be the best targets because they were filled with foreigners, particularly after 9 pm. However, as patrons didn't carry backpacks into the nightclubs, it was considered high risk. As an alternative, they considered McDonald's, Burger King, Pizza Hut, tattoo parlours and souvenir stalls as places popular with tourists where they could carry a backpack bomb without raising suspicion. Ultimately though, it was decided that restaurants in Kuta and Jimbaran Bay would be the best places to attack because they were crowded with foreigners.

Jimbaran Bay was decided as being the primary target because of the high density of dining tables, most within a metre of each other, and the men's observation had been that 80 per cent of the customers were white people. This made it a target-rich environment where multiple deaths were certain. Undoubtedly delighted at the prospect of killing so many foreigners, some of which were bound to be Australian, Azhari

THE WEDDING PLANNERS

decided to divide his resources by attacking two locations simultaneously: two in Jimbaran Bay and two in Kuta.

Critical to their plan was getting the bombs into Bali undetected. Their reconnaissance mission had identified that after arriving by ferry at the Balinese port of Gilimanuk, passengers were processed through an identity card check and luggage search. However, the search was only of the luggage being carried by each passenger; personal luggage on the bus remained unchecked. They had found the perfect loophole.

After the interviews were conducted, Azhari spent several hours developing and typing out a time-critical attack plan for the four bombers. He was methodical in his madness, as was demonstrated by the shrapnel modules he made for each backpack. To assemble these, he used a pencil and ruler to draw a precisely measured grid pattern on each of the four plastic (lunchbox-size) containers. Then, using tweezers, he selected individual steel ball bearings, dipped each into a container of glue, then precisely placed them into position on the grid; a process Azhari repeated hundreds of times for each shrapnel module until it was full of ball bearings glued into a three-dimensional death matrix. It wasn't about neatness; it was about killing efficiency.

At some stage while staying at the Batu villa, Ayip Hidayat drafted his own attack plan on a piece of A4 notepaper. Not only was he the youngest of the four bombers, he was the least educated and it's possible he wanted to impress Azhari with his own plan. We also know that Ayip Hidayat's plan used code names, precise timings and was aimed at blowing up the Ubud Art Market, two restaurants in Kuta and the next Bali victim memorial ceremony.

The commemoration for the first Bali bombing was to be held on 12 October 2005. The ceremony would have been an ideal target as it was always attended by high-profile dignitaries from Indonesia and Australia, bombing victims and victims' families, and hundreds of caring Indonesians and Australians. As if any additional incentive was needed, during the multi-faith ceremony Hindu and Christian prayers were held.

In the final stages of planning, however, Azhari decided there would only be three suicide bombers, Ayip Hidayat, Misno and Salik – Anif was removed from his plan. This may have been because Anif had proven a useful asset for Azhari, or he simply wasn't 'ready' – his Islamic kill-switch wasn't sufficiently wired.

Regardless of his reasoning, sitting at the wooden table in the dimly lit dining area, Azhari informed the group that the three-bomb attack was planned for 1 October 2005 – four days away. Ayip Hidayat was nominated to attack Raja's Bar and Restaurant in Kuta; Salik, the Nyoman restaurant in Jimbaran; and Misno, the Menega Cafe also in Jimbaran. The school friends would suicide together.

THE WEDDING PLANNERS

Azhari handed the men a printed page from his Bali Bomb Project document with the title, 'The Attack'. The below passage has been translated directly from that document:

5.25 pm – Pack, check out of the boarding house and synchronise watches.

5.30 pm – Look for a motorcycle taxi to Legion Beach in Kuta.

6.15 pm – Arrive near the Hard Rock Cafe and look for a place to pray.

6.35 pm – End evening prayers. Then the two groups split up.

7.21 pm – The man who is going to detonate his explosives in Kuta begins moving toward the restaurant, making sure the red and green lights are on.

7.33 pm – Make sure the delay switches are all ready, and enter the restaurant.

Meanwhile, the other two suicide bombers arrive at Jimbaran beach at 6.50 pm (by motorcycle taxi) and wait at a food stall until 7.30 pm. Then synchronise their watches again. Begin walking along the beach to the outdoor tables, one 45 metres behind the other. The first man walks into the table area (Menega cafe) and the second man does the same (Nyoman café).

7.34 pm – *Allahu Akbar!!!*

DEFEATING TERROR

Over the next few days Ayip Hidayat, Salik and Misno studied the plan and prepared for their mission. They also recorded their last will and testaments. This was a great opportunity to capture some Islamic propaganda, which could later be published on the internet to inspire other would-be fanatics. After this, the men changed their traditional Muslim appearance so they would blend into Bali's tourist scene. Freshly shaved and wearing Western-style T-shirts, jeans and thongs, the men set off on their one-way trip.

PART THREE

THE SIN OF BIN

BRAIN TASER

2 October 2005

Five days after the trio set off from Azhari's villa and 24 hours after their murderous explosions killed 20 people, I was sitting at my Canberra desk, red-eyed and rummaging through the last few pages of the JI Intelligence Package – Part Two and the daily intelligence report. It was 11 pm: a long day, but it wasn't over yet. The momentum of the investigation and information flowing to me was unrelenting. Emails with attached reports kept the bold Unread Emails alert on my screen rotating like the odometer on a speeding car.

I looked over and the vault employee was looking incredibly bored. However, when I grabbed the red satchel off my desk, he sprang like a sprinter from starting blocks, key in hand. In one smooth movement, he slid the coarse zip closed and padlocked it to its anchor. 'Okay,' he said as if he had somewhere else to be urgently – like his home. He about-faced and paced like a prison escapee toward the freedom of my office door.

DEFEATING TERROR

'Is there any more information, anything at all?' I asked.

He froze, caught by the verbal prison searchlight. Without turning around, he replied, 'That's everything. You've read everything.'

'If anything new arrives, can you bring it to me straight away please.'

'Sure,' he said – and the pause button on his legs was released.

Despite the frenetic flow of information from the Bali Forward Command Post and the Incident Coordination Centre in Canberra, and the less-than-subtle pressure from AFP management, at this stage I was feeling relatively more comfortable. I had rapidly doubled my knowledge about JI and their latest attack methodologies. However, I didn't have the advantage of knowing the detail contained in Azhari's 'Bali Project' document – it wouldn't be found for weeks.

Unaware of its existence, the best I could do was rely on the intelligence from JI's previous attacks. This told me that, while JI had previously used smaller devices, they had a preference for vehicle-borne bombs in vans. They had planned to do this in Singapore in 2001, and the organisation continued with the same technique using van bombs in Bali in 2002, at the Jakarta Marriott in 2003 and the Australian embassy in 2004.

I also knew that since 2001, the bulk of their explosive packages used ammonium nitrate (a highly effective explosive

BRAIN TASER

fertiliser) usually with a smaller pre-charge of TNT. After bulk ammonium nitrate explodes it leaves telltale traces around the scene that can be analysed.

I had also learned their devices relied upon three methods for detonation: a delayed timing circuit, an immediate detonation circuit and remote detonation by mobile phone.

Most of this information conflicted with crime scene reports I was receiving from the Forward Command Post in Bali. Unfortunately, sitting at the head of a complex international investigation such as this is not like watching *NCIS*, *CSI* or *Law & Order*. In real-life large-scale investigations that are in the national media spotlight, gigabytes of information flow in from well-meaning members of the public, witnesses, those that think they are witnesses, interest groups, academics, self-declared terrorism experts, the mentally unbalanced and also malicious pranksters. Some of this information is critically useful, but most is not. All this information needs to be fact-checked and, where possible, independently corroborated before it's combined with the information flowing in from police investigation teams. As such, a significant amount of the investigative effort is spent on discounting false, misleading and fabricated information, rather than following a neat set of clues that lead you directly to the perpetrator as television would have us believe.

My comparative analysis between the current Bali crime scenes and previous JI crime scenes had raised more questions

DEFEATING TERROR

than it answered. While logic indicated it was an Islamic terror attack, I needed to remain objective. At the time of the second Bali attack, JI was not the only active terror organisation in Indonesia and no claim of responsibility had been made by them, as occurred immediately after their last bombing of the Australian embassy. From the three crime scenes, there were no traces of ammonium nitrate, a signature of JI's previous attacks. So, to side with public opinion and automatically assume JI was behind the bombing could have been a critical error, resulting in wasted time and resources and a disservice to the victims.

What I didn't know at the time, what in fact no one outside Azhari's *Thoifah Muqatilah* group knew, was that Azhari's methods had evolved again. He had deliberately and cunningly made wholesale changes to JI's previous attack modus operandi. By design this was meant to take the victims and intelligence agencies by surprise, and to frustrate the subsequent police investigation by extinguishing leads that had previously exposed members of the group.

Azhari had learned from the first Bali bombing and the Marriott and Australian embassy attacks that large vehicle-borne devices leave too many leads for the police to follow: large bombs required the purchase of hefty amounts of chemicals, which can be traced, and the vehicle itself must be registered. Additionally, from a technical perspective, it's very difficult

BRAIN TASER

to get a large device to explode completely efficiently. So the detonation of a large bomb, particularly one inside a vehicle, leaves residue that can be forensically examined to determine the composition of the explosive mix, providing more leads for the police. On top of that, the preparation of such a device needs a house in which to construct and mix the chemicals, and this too can leave a goldmine of evidence.

For this attack, Azhari had deliberately decided to use bombs carried by people rather than vehicles. He had also used TNT as the main explosive because it burns far more efficiently than the ammonium nitrate bombs he'd used in the past. Critically, for the first time Azhari had not connected or used a mobile phone to detonate the devices, as this had previously left physical evidence (phone and SIM card) and also a technical footprint (electronic call and movement data) for the police to trace. So, the team I assigned to analyse the pattern, movement and connections of the many thousands of phones in Bali that were active just prior to the time Raja's was attacked until the instant the last bomb was detonated in Jimbaran Bay were looking for something that simply wasn't there. Similarly, because of the efficiency of TNT, nor was there adequate amounts of blast residue from the three sites that could be quickly analysed in the field. Minuscule explosive traces had been found, but these required both laboratory analysis outside Indonesia and time – a luxury in short supply.

At the end of my 31-hour shift I walked along the dimly lit Northbourne Avenue, wheeling my hastily packed luggage towards the hotel I was yet to book into. I was tired, needed a shower and definitely needed a sleep, but my brain was still wired to the investigation and my ears were ringing with the very pointed 'please explain' questions from management. I ran through everything that had occurred and was confident that I had the right people with the right skills in the right places.

I knew Detachment 88 would be working tirelessly, and the AFP now had more than 100 agents working extremely hard in Australia and overseas, but we had made little progress identifying the bombers, despite their heads being the morbid centrepieces of each crime scene. This would have been less of an issue in a smaller, more bureaucratic country. However, in a country of 240 million people where medical and dental records are either paper-based files or simply non-existent, in the absence of someone personally identifying one of the heads it was an immense challenge.

The management thumbscrews were also being wound tighter to identify the network that supported the bombers. While Top and Azhari were lead suspects, a concerted effort by Indonesian and Australian police had failed to locate and arrest either over the last three years. Regardless, a result was wanted, and expected.

BRAIN TASER

As I walked along, I was internally scanning through a mental checklist and was deeply in thought when my phone rang.

'Hey Ice,' the voice said, using the call sign I'd carried since I was a recruit.

It had nothing to do with being cool, brave or heroic in any way. It was simply a product of having a sauna (and a few beers) with a few of my Mediterranean mates, whose ability to sweat profusely was second-to-none. By comparison, I hardly sweat at all; hence, 'Iceman' and other derivatives remained my nomenclature for the next two decades.

I recognised the deep gravelly voice immediately. It was Sam, a close friend and colleague. After the first Bali bombing in 2002, he'd transferred to one of the secret unnamed joint INP–AFP terror tracking teams, pursuing JI operatives throughout Indonesia. Because of the covert nature of the work, I hadn't heard from him for months.

'Hi mate, how are you?' I asked.

Ignoring my question, he replied, 'They put you in charge of counterterrorism and look what you let happen.'

'I know mate, I've just got a knack for being in the hot seat.'

'In case you didn't know, I'm working in the Forward Command Post in Bali. You've gotta come over here mate, you can't investigate from there.'

DEFEATING TERROR

Sam was always one to call a spade a spade, and I knew exactly what he meant. It was particularly frustrating relying on written reports and phone calls and being thousands of kilometres away from the crime scenes. I had full confidence in everyone in Bali and knew that they were working hard in providing me with all the critical information. Regardless, it was like investigating by remote control, something I wasn't used to.

'Sam I'd love to get over there mate, but you know senior management need a head in Canberra to kick for all the mistakes you blokes are making over there,' I said sarcastically.

'Despite your general incompetence, you'll do a good job, Ice – let me know if you need anything,' Sam had a natural ability to be able to insult and support someone simultaneously.

'No worries, just don't let any more bombs go off for fuck's sake.'

I picked up a juicy kebab from a greasy takeaway shop, then booked into the hotel and entered the sanctuary of the room. After setting my alarm for 5.30 am – six glorious hours away – I devoured the kebab, showered and fell into a sporadic sleep. While I felt a great sense of relief that the injured Australians were getting all the medical assistance and support they needed, I was far from satisfied with the investigation.

Perhaps it was my natural sense of justice, or perhaps it was even vengeance on behalf of the dead and injured, but I wanted

BRAIN TASER

more than anything to see the perpetrators locked up and for their killing to stop. I knew I couldn't rest, psychologically at least, until that happened.

I had a few phone calls during the night from the ICC and the Forward Command Post, asking for guidance and to provide me with critical updates. So, when the 5.30 alarm prodded me into partial consciousness, the best I could do was make my way, zombie-like, into the shower and let the water do the rest.

One hour, two Panadol and a double shot of black coffee later, I was sitting at my desk preparing the morning briefing paper for senior management. By 7.30 am, I had fully rebounded and was ready for the day.

About this time, I received an email with the day's press clippings attached. When I clicked the attachment, I was shocked by what I saw. The Indonesian police, who were also under significant pressure for a breakthrough, had released graphic colour photos of the three suicide bombers' heads to the media during the night. They were appealing for public assistance with identifying the perpetrators.

Two of the heads at best looked like they had been savagely ripped off horizontally at the neck; the third, chainsawed diagonally from the upper neck across to under the opposite arm pit, leaving the shoulder and mutilated arm attached. All of them looked like they had been at the losing end of a fight

173

with a pack of pitbulls. I had seen the photos the day before as part of the investigation, but I certainly didn't expect to see them in the media.[107]

The Indonesian police were the lead agency for the investigation: it was their country, their jurisdiction and predominantly their citizens who were the victims. However, since the Bali One bombing a very close, trusting relationship between the INP and AFP had flourished. This made it easy to coordinate and combine Indonesian and Australian resources and share lines of investigation and intelligence very closely. However, the decision to publish the photos took me totally by surprise. What wasn't surprising was that no one had come forward to identify the macabre, distorted and discoloured heads – I doubted that even their own mothers could have done so.

That morning I spoke with one of the AFP's leading forensic officers and asked if it was possible to reshape the heads so they could be returned to a more recognisable state. If this was possible, then we could re-photograph and republish the photos, increasing the chance of identification. In the event of relatives not coming forward to identify the heads, I was also hoping to use facial recognition software to conduct a comparative analysis between the reconstructed heads and photographic databases, such as drivers' licences, identity cards, etc. It would then also be possible to match the faces to fake or legitimate forms of identification and CCTV footage in Bali.

BRAIN TASER

The forensic officer thought I was being ambitious and wasn't confident the accuracy of the reconstruction would achieve what was required for facial recognition software. However, she was confident the general appearance would be very close. After gaining consent from the INP, I sent forensic officers to undertake the painstaking, gory, but necessary task.

Later that same day we had our first breakthrough. On the night of the bombing, Gary Shaw, from Batemans Bay, had been video recording as he walked along with his family and friends outside Raja's. His recording inadvertently picked up Hidayat (from a back view), wearing a black shirt, jeans and a backpack, walking quickly into the restaurant and then exploding.

Despite some witnesses stating that bombs had been thrown into the restaurant areas, I suspected either vests or backpack devices, because the three heads had been severed from their torsos at each crime scene. Gary Shaw's footage confirmed the latter. We also now knew the brand of backpack and that could lead enquiries to where it may have been purchased.

It also provided identification of the clothing the bomber was wearing that night, which would assist with separating his remains from those of the innocent. While the footage didn't show his face, so we still had no 'lifelike' face for identification purposes, it was unprecedented to have such clear footage of a suicide attack. As I was busy with strategic matters, such as the twice-daily IDETF meetings, management briefings and

DEFEATING TERROR

providing guidance to the ICC and Forward Command Post, I assigned an investigation team in Canberra to assess the footage. So it wasn't until late that night in my office that I actually got to review the footage in person.

During the day, the investigation team assigned to assess the clip had come up with several minor leads, which were now assigned to federal agents, but nothing significant. I wanted to be satisfied that nothing had been missed, so I watched the clip over and over again, desperately seeking any additional clues. I played it frame by frame forwards and backwards. I isolated the audio track and listened to that several times without visual distraction, then I did the opposite, many times. My obsessive determination for results had the one-minute clip consuming almost two hours at the end of my lengthy shift. Nothing. I couldn't come up with one lead that the team hadn't already suggested.

By 11 pm I was once again walking along Northbourne Avenue towards the hotel. Fatigued and clutching a McDonald's meal in one hand and my briefcase in the other, I walked along the concrete path replaying the Raja's video in my mind. I couldn't believe it had failed to yield any major breakthrough for the investigation. I was sure there must have been something in it. But there wasn't.

Just before 5.30 am, I was deeply asleep enjoying the soundtrack of the rattling air-conditioner in the wall when

BRAIN TASER

suddenly my brain was hit by a taser. The electric thought made me spring bolt upright in bed. There *was* something we had missed. After rinsing my face and donning a pair of jeans and a polo shirt, I trekked quickly back to AFP headquarters. I watched the clip again. There it was. In the very first few frames of the clip, the bomber's right arm was being lifted slightly vertically from the waist, before resuming the usual back-and-forth swing in synchronisation with his walk. It may have been the case that out of the camera's view, he had just placed something in his right rear jeans pocket.

One of the basic measures taught to suicide bombers is to either carry nothing that can identify them after the bombing, or at the very least to place identification cards and documents with the bomb to guarantee their destruction. If he had placed something in his pocket, it was possible that, because the blast direction from the backpack was above his waistline, the 'something' had not been totally destroyed. It could produce an abundance of clues.

By 7 am I had sent a detailed tasking sheet to the Forward Command Post regarding the Raja's crime scene, focused predominantly on locating any wallet, document or other article that could be DNA-matched to the bomber or that had fibres attached that matched the cloth of his jeans.

Feeling satisfied that we now had a new avenue of enquiry, I was walking to the lifts, admittedly looking tired, unshaven and casual, when one of the senior managers walked into the foyer. He was dressed in a pristine suit and tie, smelling of fresh aftershave and carrying a coffee. The manager looked me up and down, flashed a look of disgust in my direction and then walked off, shaking his head.

It was as if he expected me to apologise for being an unpleasant sight. While he had been sleeping many AFP and INP officers had been working throughout the night. I wanted to drop that smarmy prick right where he stood ... and take his coffee.

I did return to the hotel for a shower and a shave before returning to work, not because the over-groomed insurance salesman wanted me to, but because I bloody well needed it to freshen up for another double shift – we had murders to solve.

THE PLOT

On 6 October 2005, the Forward Command Post staff successfully located a partial wallet amongst the rubble at Raja's. The wallet had been burnt and torn by the blast. However, denim threads from the bomber's jeans were found melted into the velcro of the wallet, successfully coupling the two items.

As I had suspected, and hoped, the bomber had placed something – a wallet – in his right rear pocket moments before the blast. Unfortunately, the wallet didn't contain any form of identification, but it did have the remains of a charred handwritten note. Due to the immense heat, the paper was now very fragile and needed to be handled with care to maintain its integrity. On the note were fragments of faint Indonesian writing and a patchy piecemeal map.[108]

As the AFP interpreters and forensic staff worked on the note, I was pacing the halls of AFP headquarters waiting for results. After four days of intensive investigation by so many officers, I was looking forward to briefing the powers-that-be on what I felt sure would be the first positive breakthrough towards identifying at least one of the bombers. Finally, the encrypted Australian government phone that linked me directly with the Forward Command Post sprang to life.

'Hello, tell me what we've got,' I said expectantly.

'You're not gonna like this.'

'Why, what does the note say?'

'As best as we can make out from all the pieces, it looks like we've uncovered another attack.'

The words delivered an unexpected uppercut. 'What!' I said, too loudly.

'It looks like there are four bombers intending to bomb the Bali anniversary commemoration planned for 12 October.'

'So I want to get this straight,' I said, thinking out loud. 'It looks like there is a clear and present intention to bomb the next Bali ceremony, in less than a week?'

'Looks like it, yeah,' the deadpan voice replied.

'You have got to be kidding me!' I stood there, stunned, thinking of the implications. Victims of the first bombing and their families would be attending; not to mention high-ranking Indonesian and Australian dignitaries, including the foreign minister, and perhaps even the prime minister.

'I wish I was,' echoed into my ear.

Ice was no Iceman – I was starting to panic. 'Keep running

THE PLOT

down every line of enquiry you can in respect to this, drop everything else that's not essential.'

'It's all essential, we're only doing essential things here,' he replied defensively.

'I know, I know. You'll just have to make this the highest priority. I'll get back to you.'[109]

I returned to my office and locked the door, seeking a few moments of deep thought before I took the information any further. If an attack did occur at the ceremony, killing dignitaries and victims' families, it would be a catastrophic nightmare. If the ceremony was called off, it would be a win for the terrorists, and significantly escalate the fear factor in Bali. It would also deny mourners the opportunity to gather and pay their respects.

I sat quietly and took stock of what had occurred in the past five days. Since volunteering to act in the position of AFP Commander of Counterterrorism three suicide attacks had occurred in Bali, killing 20 people and injuring hundreds more. Unlike previous bombings, the tactics used in these attacks were unprecedented and designed specifically to frustrate an investigation. It had been five days since the attacks and we had no idea who the suicide bombers were. Media reports were becoming increasingly critical about the lack of progress in the investigation. At the direction of the prime minister, the investigation now also included enquiries into multiple reports of

DEFEATING TERROR

people being forewarned about those attacks. There had also been SMS messages warning of a second attack. Now after five days of furious investigation by hundreds of people, both in the INP and AFP, we had uncovered a terrorist plot to murder attendees at the Bali One commemoration ceremony in six days' time. A plan that seemed to corroborate the SMS messages. People talk about policing being a stressful career – this is a good example of it.

Everyone's stress levels would have been lowered if we only knew that what we had actually uncovered was Hidayat's handwritten plan to attack the Ubud art market, two restaurants in Kuta and the Bali One memorial ceremony – when it was planned to use four bombers (before Anif was removed from the planning by Azhari). It was the plan Azhari didn't use. Without the benefit of this information, I sent more people to Bali and we continued to investigate every avenue of the Bali bombings that had occurred – and those that were now expected.

Despite an intensely concerted effort over the following days by more than 40 Indonesian and Australian assets, we hadn't been able to find one concrete lead in support of the written plan, the forewarning rumours or the SMS messages. Just days before the Bali One ceremony, a combined investigation and a classified intelligence threat assessment cleared the path for the commemoration to go ahead. By midday 12 October 2005, I was glad the morning ceremony had proceeded with the respect, dignity and peace those attending deserved.

HEADS, YOU WIN

After many hours of painstaking work, the talented forensic officers had completed the gruesome task of restoring the bombers' heads. Indonesian police then photographed and re-published the images: this time they looked lifelike, and less demonic. Within days, we had a flood of people coming forward and volunteering they recognised, or thought they recognised, the bombers' heads. This led police to several family interviews in Java, Sumatra, Bali and Lombok, where they also took DNA samples from the houses for comparison with the heads.

Pursuing one such lead, Indonesian police attended the village of Cidulang in the Majalengka district of Java. There they interviewed a community member who identified the Nyoman bomber as a man who had been selling clothing in the local markets for some time, but in August he simply disappeared. The community member hadn't been completely convinced by the first round of Indonesian police photos. However, when the second set of photos was distributed, he was sure it was Salik Firdaus, a father of one child and the youngest of six siblings.

As a child, Salik Firdaus had been raised and educated in Islamic boarding schools that bred hatred and intolerance.[110] Some in Majalengka described him as a religious fanatic who had preached radical Islam for many years in the district. While some in the marketplace had suspected he was one of the bombers, they felt it would bring too much shame on the village to come forward. However, when shown photos of the reconstructed heads by police, their wilful blindness was washed away and they had no choice but to identify him and where he lived.

Police then visited Salik's family home. Days later, the DNA samples that were taken were successfully matched to the head in the sand at the Nyoman restaurant. This confirmed Salik Firdaus as the Nyoman restaurant bomber. Now finally, after three weeks, we had a win.

I took this new information to a senior management meeting on the executive floor. As I entered the oval-shaped room the thick grey curtains were drawn around its circumference, covering the large segmented glass wall. With some disdain, I noticed the insurance salesman I had encountered in the foyer was among those taking a seat around the polished table. In turn, each gave an update on the pressing issues in their respective portfolios.

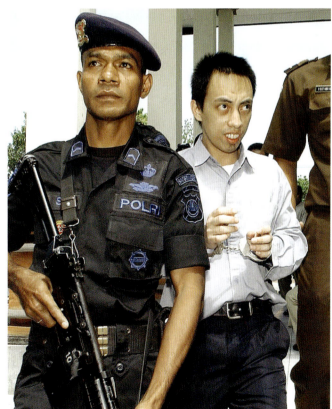

Above: After his capture Indonesian Muhammad Cholili is interrogated by AFP officer David Craig and his Indonesian counterparts as they investigate the bombings.

Right: A policeman escorts Cholili to a court room for his trial in Denpasar, Bali, in August 2006. (SONNY TUMBELAKA/AFP/Getty Images)

Above: Australian Minister for Foreign Affairs Alexander Downer speaks during the memorial service held on 12 October 2005 in Kuta to mark the anniversary of the 2002 Bali bombings. The investigation into the Bali bombings of 2005 is in full swing and the AFP are on high alert for the ceremony. (JASON CHILDS/Getty Images)

Below: The many faces of Malaysian Dr Azhari one of the main suspects in the Bali bombing investigations. (BAY ISMOYO/AFP/Getty Images)

Above: Australian Federal Police officer David Craig discusses the anthrax investigation with Indonesia's ambassador, Imron Cotan.

Below: Newspaper reports of the suspected anthrax attack.

Above: AFP officer David Craig discusses the progress of the 2005 Bali bombings investigation with senior INP officer Gilang (identity disguised) in Indonesia.

Below: The news breaks of Azhari's death in the *Jakarta Post*. The Islamic radical blew himself up after being cornered by armed police inside a house in the East Java town of Batu. Azhari was the mastermind behind the four deadly terrorist attacks in Indonesia.

Above: The ruins of Azhari's bomb factory hideout in Batu where Azhari was planning more attacks after the 2005 Bali bombing. (Getty Images)

Below: Indonesian forensic police discover bomb-making materials, Azhari's records and a laptop at the site of the police raid in Batu. (DIMAS ARDIAN/Getty Images)

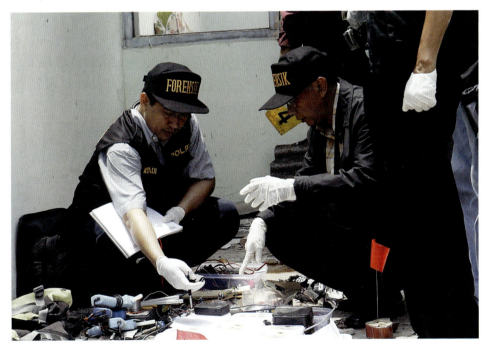

Above: In newspaper reports the Indonesian bomb squad is depicted leaving the site of Azahari's death after giving the all clear.

Below: A policeman guards Islamic militant Iwan Darmawan Mutho, alias Rois, before his trial in South Jakarta. Rois was charged with plotting the deadly bombing at the Australian Embassy in Jakarta. Rois told police that Al-Qaeda leader Osama bin Laden had funded the attack. (BAY ISMOYO/AFP/Getty Images)

Following their arrest Indonesians Anif Solchanudin (above) and Abdul Azis (below) are escorted by officials at the prosecutor's office in Denpasar in March 2006. (SONNY TUMBELAKA/AFP/Getty Images)

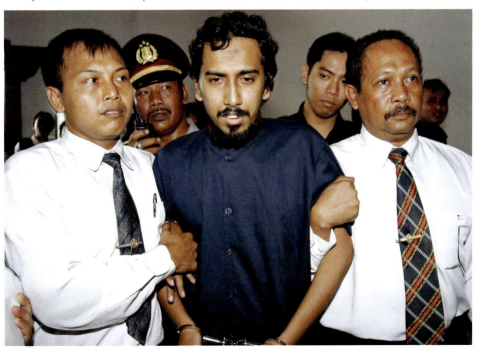

Left: A local shows David Craig where Azhari was trapped by police in 2005.

Middle: The gunshots fired during the firefight are still evident.

Below: In 2017 David Craig marks the spot where Azhari's body was found after the Batu shootout.

HEADS, YOU WIN

When it was my turn, I provided the details of the Salik Firdaus breakthrough. When I finished, one of the junior managers who I'd not met before said, 'That's good that you've identified one of the three bombers. But there's still another two. How long until we'll know who they are?'

'Well I'm convinced that now we've identified Salik Firdaus, that we'll be able to run down enquiries surrounding his movements since August and identify his accomplices,' I said optimistically.

Then the insurance salesman chimed in. 'You still don't know where Azhari is, do you?' he demanded, making me feel like I'd been ambushed.

His question, which was more of an accusation, caught me by surprise. I was tired and it pissed me off. In my mind I yelled, *Teams of people have spent the last three years trying to locate Azhari, and now I'm meant to have found him in three weeks, while investigating the three bombing attacks, the rumours, the SMS messages and also prevent another bombing?*

I took a deep breath and thought, *No, David. Calm,* and I replied professionally, albeit through tight lips: 'No, we've been focusing on other aspects mainly. We have one team dedicated to finding him because he remains our major suspect, but considering the difficulties in the past, I think the strongest chance of us finding him is through new developments from the current investigation. So that's been where we've been predominantly focused.'

'Well we need to speed the results up. The minister, the prime minister, the public are all expecting an outcome.'

My blood started to boil but I restrained myself. 'I want an outcome as much as anyone else, but it's just slow, painstaking and frustrating work. I'm the senior investigating officer and I'm trying to lead it from another country. I know in theory having the information emailed to me and having photos sent should be enough. But it's not, not for me. I need to get on the ground in Indonesia. I need the personal interaction with investigators, I want to hear what they have to say, what they think, see the crime scenes, not just be emailed sanitised reports twice daily. I want to grab this investigation by the horns but it's hard to do from another country.'

I paused my rant, realising that the room was suddenly very quiet and I had a lot of eyes on me.

'Okay, pack your bags and make the travel arrangements. You'll need to fly to Jakarta first to get an in-country intelligence briefing, then fly to Bali and take command of the Forward Command Post,' said the most senior manager in the room.

I couldn't believe it. It was as simple as that.

'Okay, thank you,' I said, too politely.

I left the room quickly in case they changed their minds. At last I would be able to immerse myself in every aspect of the investigation. Like every other operation I'd led, I needed to

HEADS, YOU WIN

see it, feel it and taste it. Yes, I'm obsessive – but I usually get results.

The following day I caught a Garuda flight to Jakarta where an AFP liaison officer met me at the airport and took me to the embassy. As we turned into the driveway I saw scorch marks on cement walls and pieces of twisted fencing outside the embassy as a result of Azhari's penultimate attack. *I am going to fucken get you,* I pledged silently to Azhari.

The following morning, before departing for Bali, someone from another Australian agency came to the AFP office to meet with me. We sat in a confined meeting room and closed the door. They're all largely the same, these grey types. They have a natural knack for condescension. Regardless, I sat there being talked at about Indonesian politics, population demographics, the economy and all manner of eclectic information that had nothing to do with my remit. Finally, 'Mr Grey' said something that caught my interest: '... so it's the case that the bilateral relationship between the INP and Badan Intelijen Negara – that's Indonesian Intelligence, or as we like to call them the BIN, ha ha – is somewhat strained of late.'[111]

If the INP had a problem, I needed to know about it – they were our most trusted partners. I smiled politely at his BIN joke then asked, 'What's caused the friction and how bad is the relationship?'

'Well let's just say it's a bit of a rocky marriage, ha ha.'

187

'We could just say that, but that doesn't mean anything does it …' I paused to allow him time to realise that I was interested in facts, not innuendo. 'Can you tell more about that and whether it affects our tactical relationship?'

As Indonesia's primary intelligence agency, I expected BIN would have swamped Bali after the bombings and be monitoring the phones and activities of all foreign government officials there. That's an understandable standard operating procedure for most countries in such a situation. It never bothered me because the AFP don't spy in foreign countries — we simply assist when invited, with law enforcement expertise. As it was a nationally significant terrorist attack, I also expected that BIN would be providing some critical intelligence support for the INP; without it the INP, and in turn the AFP, could be missing some vital information that might assist with the investigation.

'Well, in my opinion the trouble started after the first Bali bombing. BIN had only been operating for a few years when it happened. It was a disaster for them. They were criticised for not briefing the Indonesian government on the rise of JI and its potential for a large bomb attack, such as occurred in Bali. On the other side of the coin the INP, who were really their poor cousins before the bombings, have now had an amazing run of success. The INP successes have resulted in a very popular public profile in the Indonesian community. Because of their popularity, the Indonesian government has increased their budget significantly. BIN are now fast becoming the poor cousins.'

I knew that ever since 9/11, in many countries law enforcement had responded by expanding their operations into more traditional intelligence areas, which had resulted in some friction between intelligence and law enforcement agencies. 'So there's inter-agency rivalry and jealousy? Nothing new in that, it happens all the time in Australia too.'

'It seems BIN and the INP have almost stopped cooperating and are now competing with each other. They work almost in isolation to each other and never share real-time intelligence,' Mr Grey said.

'Really? It'd be extremely difficult to effectively investigate terrorism without law enforcement and intelligence agencies cooperating and sharing information and resources.'

I made a mental note to tread carefully with the INP around the subject of intelligence support and BIN, as Mr Grey went on to other matters.

Late that afternoon, the Garuda Airlines flight I was on bumped down onto Denpasar's airstrip and taxied to a stop. As soon as I stepped out of the aircraft's doorway, the familiar smell and humidity brought back a slideshow of happy memories that played as I walked across the tarmac under the bloodshot sky.

I was met by Sam.

'How ya goin, Champion? About time you got here. No midday naps here mate, it's not Canberra.' Typical.

Sam hadn't changed. It was good to see his trademark two-gauge almost-shaved haircut, and goatee beard complete with a half-smoked cigarette balancing expertly from one side.

'Well Sam, I don't know what you blokes have been doing over here. Bugger-all by the look of your tan. Pool nice is it?' I asked sarcastically.

There would be a few people in the Forward Command Post that I didn't know, but I did know Sam. The glassy roadmaps in his eyes weren't concealed by the wisps of smoke from his cigarette, nor by the crow's-feet created by his teasing smile. It was clear that he had been working untold hours, as I knew he would have been.

With the remnants of my previous Bali holiday arrivals still swirling through my mind, it felt incongruous, awkward and almost deceitful to be walking out of the airport terminal building with an aluminium combination-locked security briefcase. I should have been lugging a backpack and under my other arm should have been a surfboard, not a sealed cylinder filled with a series of A1-sized crime intelligence charts. Sam led the way to the waiting white Tarago van.

'This is Ketut, he's been hired as the Forward Command Post driver. He's available 24/7, aren't you Ketut?'

HEADS, YOU WIN

'Yes, wherever you want to go I can take you,' the middle-aged Balinese driver said cheerfully as he helped put the luggage into the back of the van.

We shook hands. 'Nice to meet you Ketut.'

'Nice to meet you, Mister Ice,' he said with a broad smile.

'Don't listen to what Sam tells you Ketut, just call me David, mate,' I said as I flashed a what-the-fuck expression at Sam, who was enjoying the moment too much.

With his Hindu goddess statue sitting proudly on the dashboard, Ketut expertly negotiated us through the chaotic traffic towards the Kartika Plaza hotel in Kuta. I'd been out of phone contact for the previous hour and a half.

'So Sam, what's the latest?'

'Well, the Kartika Plaza's received another two threatening phone calls today, three yesterday, all to do with them allowing Australian police to stay there.'

'Hmmm, probably a result of us identifying Firdaus. Has the personnel security officer updated and reviewed the staff threat assessment and premises security plan?' I wondered aloud. 'Anything else?'

'Yeah, the INP has sent a new boss to take over in Bali. He arrived this morning. Probably because the AFP have sent you, they want to have someone at your equivalent rank in the Forward Command Post, just to keep things even.'

'Really? Is it someone you know, what's his name?'

191

'I'd never met him, because I've been in the field for months. He seems like a good bloke. He's from Detachment 88 in Jakarta, apparently, he's one of their new rising stars.'

'Does the star have a name?'

'Gilang Herianto.'[112]

A wave of happiness washed over me. 'Perfect.'

ANTHRAX & FLOWERS

Canberra, 1 June 2005 (four months earlier)

Late in the afternoon, Prime Minister John Howard fronts a packed media conference. He's not happy.

'It's an act of reckless indifference to human life and I apologise on behalf of the Australian people to the Indonesian embassy and government … It's still being tested … it's not an innocent white powder, it's some kind of biological agent …'[113]

Earlier that day a staff member at the Indonesian embassy in Australia had opened a letter addressed to Indonesia's ambassador, Imron Cotan. As she did so, white powder spilt out across the desk and her lap. Seconds later, the white cloud entered the embassy air conditioning, contaminating the entire building. The incident sparked a well-practised emergency response that had been honed over the previous few years, as a result of multiple hoax anthrax letters in Australia and overseas.

The contents of these letters almost invariably ended up being household flour, but this occasion was different. After emergency services evacuated and sealed the embassy, a field test was carried out on the powder. This time, it tested positive as a biological agent from the bacillus group, possibly anthrax.

This had never occurred in Australia and news of the incident flooded national and international media. It was promptly labelled as Australia's first 'bio-terror' attack. Indonesia's president, Susilo Bambang Yudhoyono, declared to the media that he considered it an attack on Indonesia itself, and that Indonesia would not be intimidated.

Some Indonesian politicians jumped at the chance to hit back at Australia's continued travel warnings of potential terrorist attacks after the Bali One bombing. Joko Sisilo (a member of Indonesia's Foreign Affairs Committee) said to the media that Indonesia should now issue a travel warning for Australia and that 'the attack proves Australians are capable of committing their own acts of terrorism'.[114]

By coincidence or not, the biological agent in the envelope was sent to the Indonesian Embassy at the precise time Schapelle Corby was appealing her 20-year sentence for drug trafficking. This fuelled Indonesian suspicion that the Corby affair had amplified some Australians' anti-Indonesian sentiment to the point of conducting a biological attack.

ANTHRAX & FLOWERS

Prime Minister Howard and President Yudhoyono had been working hard to negotiate through the difficult political terrain following the sentencing of Corby who, to some Australians, appeared innocent. To most Indonesians, though, she was simply an international drug mule. At a time when relations between the two countries were already strained, the 'bio-attack' on the Indonesian embassy had the potential to sink the bilateral relationship to an all-time low.

AFP senior management quickly recognised that what had been a routine community policing response now had significant international ramifications. This escalated when Prime Minister Howard invited Indonesia to send police to assist with the investigation.

Someone in senior management either hated me or liked me. I had been working my way through a pile of paperwork in my Cairns office when the phone rang.

'Have you seen the media in relation to the Indonesian embassy attack?' the businesslike senior officer blurted from the other end.

'Yes. Looks like the real thing this time.'

'The prime minister has cleared the way for the Indonesian police to form part of a joint investigation taskforce we're assembling in Canberra. This is the first time that Indonesian police have been invited to investigate in Australia. With the Corby matter before the Indonesian courts, and people

195

protesting about it here, you can ascertain for yourself that this is a high-profile matter with significant political sensitivities.'

'Sounds like a minefield,' I said, excited by the prospect of being part of the joint investigation.

'We'd like you to come to Canberra tonight and lead the joint task force, okay?'

'Absolutely,' I said as I looked at the stack of boring paperwork on my desk.

'Good. You'll be given a briefing tomorrow morning in Canberra. The Indonesians arrive in the afternoon.'

Excitement and anticipation were running in my veins when I arrived at AFP Canberra headquarters. The Indonesian embassy remained closed, with 22 of its staff still being kept in isolation. Over the next hour I was given a briefing. Then I was told that three INP officers and a representative from the Indonesian Ministry of Agriculture would be arriving to form part of the investigation task force that afternoon.[115]

'I understand why they are sending INP officers, but why someone from the Indonesian Ministry of Agriculture?' I asked the briefing officer.

'I know, it's strange but it's their choice. Perhaps he's a spy,' she said, tongue in cheek.

Late that afternoon, with AFP senior management, I met with the four Indonesians at the Winchester Police Centre in front of a significant media contingent. After the media

ANTHRAX & FLOWERS

conference, when the cameras and their crews had disappeared, I sat down with the Indonesians and we introduced ourselves over cups of tea and coffee.

The most senior INP officer was a jovial bear of a man who could have easily fitted into the forward pack of a Fijian rugby team. With a head the size of a ripe watermelon and a smile to match, you couldn't help but like him from the outset. His name was Gilang Herianto and he spoke fluent English, as did one of the other INP officers, Harta.[116] Harta was a short, slightly built man with a polite, almost submissive demeanour. This was exaggerated by the softly spoken words that wisped from his mouth fronted by white teeth and a single gold fascia.

The other INP officer, Prendy, and the representative from the Ministry of Agriculture, Kuwat, didn't speak English.[117] Fortunately, during the six months I spent with the United Nations in East Timor I had been able to extend my rudimentary Bahasa Indonesian language skills. While that was four years prior, I retained some basic Indonesian conversational skills and did my best to communicate politely with the two of them.

I stepped them through the investigation, pausing regularly to allow Gilang to explain the details in Indonesian. The three INP officers asked questions throughout my explanation. Conversely, Kuwat, from the Ministry of Agriculture, remained silent and appeared aloof, almost disconnected from the conversation. *Maybe he really is a spy*, I thought as I discreetly continued to observe his demeanour.

After introducing the Indonesians to the rest of the AFP team, I drove them to the Forensic Services building at Weston Creek, so they could see the envelope and the accompanying letter. Again, the INP officers were very interested and asked astute deductive questions in relation to the items. Kuwat remained awkwardly silent as I summed up the situation.

'The envelope is postmarked from Victoria so that's the main thrust of our investigation, trying to back-trace its origin.[118] We're processing the letter and the envelope for DNA and fingerprints. While the initial test showed the presence of a biological agent, I've been told it's highly unlikely to be anthrax. It's going to take about 48 hours in the laboratory to fully test the powder for spores. I suspect it's simply talcum powder or flour as is usually the case.'

Suddenly, Kuwat sprang to life and spoke up (via Gilang), 'What type of flour is it?'

'We're not sure. It could be plain, self-raising or something else. Once it's been cleared as safe by the biohazard chemists, we'll be able to conduct a full analysis so we can trace it back through the milling process. But there's over 80 flour and grain mills in Australia, so it's going to be a tough line of enquiry.'

'But surely you must know already what kind of flour it is,' Kuwat replied (via Gilang), unconvinced by my answer.

ANTHRAX & FLOWERS

'Honestly, we don't know yet.'

'But surely you could tell by the leaves and the bloom itself,' Gilang said, confusing me completely.

The four Indonesians then talked amongst themselves briefly, then Gilang turned to me and said with his infectious smile, 'It looks like there has been a misunderstanding.'

'I'm sorry Gilang, I don't understand,' I said, perplexed.

Gesturing at his agricultural colleague, Gilang then exploded into laughter but managed to get out, 'You see, we were told in Jakarta that the envelope would probably have a flower in it. Flower like in a garden, not like they use to make bread.'

Then the penny dropped and I joined in the circle of laughing Indonesians. It turns out that the 'spy' was in fact a horticultural expert sent to assist identifying the type of flower, not flour.

During the following weeks, I formed a close personal and professional bond with both Gilang and Harta, despite them being polar opposites in some ways. Gilang was a beefy gregarious man who described himself as 'relaxed Christian', religiously similar to myself. Whereas Harta was a quietly spoken 'moderate Muslim'. The three of us had a lot in common: each of us was married, with young children, and tried hard to balance our commitment to law enforcement and to our families, with the former winning too often. Despite our national, cultural and religious differences, we also had shared moral views of right and wrong, the desire to catch criminals and, importantly, a similar sense of humour.

31 October 2005

Four months later in Bali, I was about to see Gilang again. The situation was reversed, though, with me being part of a foreign police contingent assisting with an investigation in *his* country.

Ketut parked the Tarago van at the front of the Kartika Plaza and walked with Sam and me to the reception area, where he found himself a comfortable chair.

'Remember Mister David Ice, any time you want to go somewhere just call me,' he said cheerfully before his head sank below the horizon of a complimentary *Jakarta Post*.

After checking in to a room I made my way to the Forward Command Post, which was situated in one of the resort's largest penthouses. The presidential suite had an expansive open lounge dining area, complete with a 12-seat extendable dining table, gourmet kitchen and four generous-sized double bedrooms. The entire suite was surrounded by panoramic floor-to-ceiling glass panels that highlighted the unobstructed views of palm trees, the white sandy beach and the sparkling blue water just 20 metres away.

The decision to book the suite had nothing to do with its obvious luxury and a lot more to do with necessity. The dining

ANTHRAX & FLOWERS

table was covered with files, phones and at least 10 laptop computers connected through the large black server sitting beside it, which provided direct real-time access to the AFP's international encrypted IT system. The lounge area was filled with office equipment ranging from photocopiers and printers to fax machines, shredders and a mobile encrypted satellite dish aimed through one of the large windows. The bedrooms had been assigned based on operational requirements: there was a forensic room, locked evidence and exhibits room, interview room and an equipment room.

I knocked on the suite's thick carved wooden door. Eventually it was opened by Sam, who led me down a hallway past the bedrooms and into the open work area. Despite there being over 30 AFP and almost as many INP working from the suite, the busy hive of activity was surprisingly well ordered. Sam, acting as a real estate guide, introduced me to staff as he showed me through the suite. Then I saw Gilang splayed out on the long leather sofa with his eyes closed. After a few seconds, he opened his eyes and laughed out, 'Hey Dave, I thought I could just sleep here in Bali now you're here to save the day.'

'Hi, Gilang, it's good to see you're still working as hard as always,' I joked as he sprang from the sofa and grabbed me in a bear hug.

He said, 'It's nice to see you Dave.'

As we patted each other's backs and separated I heard, 'Did you bring us any flowers?'

Then I looked over and I saw Harta's beaming smile on the other side of the room. 'Sorry, mate, I forgot your flowers.'

The warm reception and what was clearly an inside joke between the three of us created some puzzled looks with both the Australian and Indonesian police in the room. It was good to see the pair of them and in a strange way I was glad that I had invested the time and commitment to build a robust rapport with the two men.

When they were in Canberra, they had been the subject of some criticism from some quarters of the Australian community which was publicised in newspapers and on the internet. Some short-sighted Australians took umbrage at the fact that we had Indonesian police investigating in Australia.

Apparently, these people had forgotten the tremendous cooperation and acceptance by Indonesian police of the AFP investigating in their country. Knowing the brotherly history between the INP and the AFP, I was quite aggressively protective of my Indonesian colleagues when they were in Australia. Now with an increasing flow of threatening phone calls being received by the Kartika Plaza due to the AFP's presence, I hoped they would return the favour.

LONG SHOTS

The next day Ketut drove Gilang, Sam, me and a couple of AFP officers to Jimbaran Bay to view the Menega Cafe and Nyoman restaurant crime scenes. Apart from the chaotic stack of broken furniture, upturned tables and crime scene tape around the Jimbaran sites, the beach had returned to normal. The other restaurants had recommenced trading and, bizarrely, I saw there were diners eating in the three restaurants between the two sealed crime scenes, just metres from where death and carnage had reigned just a month before.

Most of the bloody remnants in the open-air bombsites had been either taken away or washed away by rain. But I wasn't there to collect forensic evidence – that process had been finished weeks before. I was there to get a first-hand perspective of the environment and to re-create in my mind exactly what happened that night.

On my laptop, I had press photos taken on the night of the attack, tourist photos taken before and after the bombings and a full series of detailed AFP forensic photos. In my briefcase, I had copies of all the first-hand witness statements that described the events that night. Using all this I was able to step through the events, first-hand, of every witness, victim and the bombers themselves.

I concentrated my efforts on the Newcastle table where three Australians were killed and many more were injured. It was a focus for me because the Newcastle families needed answers and because they had been deliberately targeted – this went to the motive of the attackers and the profile of people they wanted to kill.

I spent several hours retracing and re-creating in my mind the events that happened that night. Obsessive, yes. Determined, even more so.

It had been a spectacularly hot day, but the continuous sea breeze and my unrelenting concentration kept me oblivious of the sun's punishment on my toasting red forearms and neck. By mid-afternoon I was satisfied that I had absorbed all there was to absorb from Jimbaran Bay. A couple of times during my examination, I looked around and saw the normality surrounding the crime scenes: the gentle waves, locals selling statues and T-shirts and tourists taking photos. It was nice to pause and breathe in the tranquillity.

It had been over three weeks since the attacks and we were coming under increasing criticism in the media for the lack

LONG SHOTS

of progress. So while the crime scene assessment had been a lengthy process, it was invaluable and allowed me to create a list of unanswered questions and, importantly, new avenues of enquiry. The criticism by the media didn't worry me – everyone was working damn hard. For me, the pressure came from my own conscience. I wanted to have a full explanation of everything that happened for the victims and their families, and I wanted to catch the bastards that did it.

We clambered back into the oven-baked Tarago, its heat amplifying the faint scent of Ketut's Hindu sandalwood sticks. I sat in the front next to him and asked, 'Okay Ketut, can you take us to Raja's please?'

'Of course, yes,' he chuckled as if I'd just delivered a funny punchline.

How are the Balinese are always so happy? I mused.

I heard one of the others in the back say, 'Haven't you had enough today?'

Then I heard Sam say, 'I reckon we won't be stopping till midnight.'

I smiled and asked Ketut to turn up the air-conditioning.

By around 4 pm, Ketut parked in Kuta Square and we walked along the busy street to the front of Raja's. Unlike the other bombsites, this attack had occurred inside the restaurant building. After being forensically processed, the restaurant had been boarded shut with large pieces of plywood. Gilang unlocked the padlock that was securing the makeshift door: 'Dave, I don't need to go in there, I've seen it before.'

'No worries mate, I don't think I'll be too long,' I said as I pried open the narrow door and stepped inside with my briefcase and laptop. In the breeze, the door suddenly swung shut, blackening the room. As I stood there silently, waiting for my eyes to adjust to the darkness, I was hit in the face with the most horrific stench I had ever experienced, causing me to gag. Without thinking much about it, I attributed the obnoxious odour to the scene being boarded shut, combined with the high temperatures of the day and all the food left to rot in the restaurant.

With my eyes now adjusted and my gag reflex under control, just, I ventured further into the restaurant, assisted by the light streaming in from the door that someone had now propped open.

With the gag tears slowly drying in my eyes, I negotiated my way around the rubble towards the back of the restaurant, retracing the steps of the bomber that I had watched on video so many times. I was about halfway to where he detonated when I noticed the floor was sticky. Instinctively, I looked down and saw I was walking in a wide stream of semidried blood and what could have been beer. Wanting to gag again, I mentally disciplined myself. *Harden up and concentrate on the job.* As I took the next step, I saw stuck on the wall in front of me like a macabre

LONG SHOTS

mural the remains of a putrid strip of human flesh. Then I saw a woven breadbasket on the floor that had been partially filled with pieces of flesh and food. Someone with good intentions had obviously attempted to clean up, but was overcome.

The smell, the site and my thoughts were too much and I involuntarily started to heave. I knew I was going to vomit, but needed to do it outside the crime scene. I desperately made my way for the salvation of fresh air and sunlight through the door. Bursting through its threshold onto the footpath, I bent over and heaved, heaved and then heaved again.

Despite not actually vomiting, my eyes were streaming and I was salivating profusely. I was bent over and fighting the urge to heave again when an Aussie family gave me a wide berth as they walked past carrying their shopping bags, clearly enjoying their holiday in Bali. I wanted to be them. Bali used to mean that to me too, but not today. Perhaps never again. I struggled to regain my composure. *Come on, get a grip! You're supposed to be a fucken superintendent.*

'You okay mate?' I heard one of the AFP officers ask.

'Yeah, I'll be fine. It was just a bit of a shock that's all.'

'Ice, you don't have to go back in there, we've got photos,' Sam said compassionately.

'I know, mate, but this is important. If I can learn just one thing we don't know already, then we'll be one step closer,' I said as I stepped back into the darkened restaurant of horrors.

DEFEATING TERROR

I managed to spend the next 40 minutes re-creating and retracing everything that happened that night, again coming up with a list of unanswered questions scribbled in my diary. Now satisfied, I stepped from the morbid tomb back into the land of the living. I threw my rubber gloves in a bin on the footpath, then sat and regained my composure over a cold drink with the others at the cafe next door.

Then I asked one of the forensic officers to measure the length of the black-and-white painted strips on the gutter on the street. Zebra-like stripes are often painted along many of Indonesia's streets and kerbs. They vary in width, so I needed to know the precise measurements on the gutter outside Raja's. Then I asked her to measure the distance between the power poles and permanent marks in the footpath that were also outside Raja's.

That night we were able to calculate precisely how fast the bomber was walking along the footpath. Then, using 30 minutes for the time component (based on the time delay setting on the backpack devices found in Bandung) we were able to draw a circle using Raja's as a centre point to use as a guide for the area where the bombers and their supervisors may have gathered prior to the bombing. From that, we commenced a search of CCTV footage available from the Raja's centre point outwards to the circumference of the area in an attempt to backtrack the yet-to-be identified Raja's bomber. The circle included most of Kuta and its resorts and hotels, including the Hard Rock Cafe,

LONG SHOTS

where they had in fact met. It was a long shot, just one of many we were taking at the time.

The following morning, Gilang asked if we still needed the Menega cafe and Nyoman restaurant crime scenes to remain sealed. If not, the restaurants would like to reopen for business that night. As there was nothing more we needed from those two sites, I agreed. However, there was something important I wanted to do that day.

About 5 pm, I invited all the AFP and INP in the Forward Command Post to dinner – at the Nyoman restaurant. Some were too nervous and stayed at the Kartika Plaza, but most obliged. We arrived at the peaceful pristine restaurant setting on the beach just as the Nyoman restaurant opened for business for the first time since it was bombed.

We walked through the restaurant building and onto the beach area to the table I had deliberately booked – the Newcastle table. It was the same one, in the same location where the Newcastle victims had dined when they were attacked on that night. The table where Jennifer Williamson and Colin and Fiona Zwolinski were murdered. The table where many innocent Australians were injured and had their lives tragically altered. The table that Salik Firdaus had deliberately targeted.

We filed around the table and took our places. The sunset and surroundings were a replica of the afternoon on 1 October 2005 when the table last filled up with Australians.

DEFEATING TERROR

I didn't know whether there were any JI sympathisers there that night, but I wanted to send a very clear signal to anyone and everyone: Australians will not be bullied or intimidated by Islamofascist terrorist cowards. You may have killed and injured some of our countrymen and women, but you have not won, nor will you ever.

Ignoring the shrapnel scratches in the furniture and our nerves, we sat and ordered a drink. Despite not having an appetite we stayed for about an hour. If anyone was observing us that night, our message was loud and clear.

In the Forward Command Post the following day, INP and AFP (who were fluent in Bahasa Indonesian) sifted through and critically analysed the many items seized from Salik's house, including handwritten letters, address books, SIM cards and a mobile phone. This established his communication with several people, predominantly Misno. Inquiries with Misno's family revealed that he'd left home in early August in search of work and hadn't been in contact since. As instructed by Azhari, Misno had dutifully left an alibi with family explaining his extended absence. By design this resulted in his family not reporting him as missing, which both frustrated the investigation and put some time and distance between himself and Azhari. Photographs of the reconstructed heads were shown to Misno's family, confirming him as the Menega Cafe bomber.

LONG SHOTS

The next afternoon, Gilang, Harta and another INP officer returned to the Forward Command Post with bags of items and documents seized from both Salik's and Misno's houses.[119] There they were photographed, photocopied, scanned and forensically processed. When this process was completed, the items were placed on a table where the details were to be entered into the investigation database the following day.

During the afternoon, the name Ayip Hidayat, of Pamarikan in Ciamis district, West Java, was noticed in seized items from both houses. This caused us to suspect this was the identity of the Raja's bomber. I rapidly included this information in the daily Investigation Briefing Paper, to satiate the powers-that-be in Canberra.[120]

By 11 pm, I'd emailed the Investigation Briefing Paper to headquarters and walked back to my room. Shortly thereafter, I fell into another restless sleep, the cinema of my mind replaying photographs, video and developments in the investigation as my subconscious constantly scoured for ways to develop the investigation.

About 2 am, I was woken by a soft knocking on my door. I sprang to my feet and before I was fully awake, I'd opened the door. There in front of me was an Indonesian man I hadn't seen before. 'You are Craig?' he asked.

'David, David Craig, yes,' I mumbled, still not fully awake.

'I have something for you, you have pen and paper?'

'Sure hang on a sec,' I said as I picked up a piece of Kartika Plaza stationery and pen.

'Write this down,' he instructed.

Now partially awake I asked, 'Who are you?'

Without answering, he read out an Indonesian mobile phone number, which I wrote down before my fatigued memory lost it forever.

'This is for Australian only. Not Densus 88.'

'What do you mean not for Detachment 88?'

'Just for Aussie only,' he repeated and he turned and walked away.

Legally, I wasn't a police officer in Indonesia. I didn't have any police powers, and I couldn't detain or question him. I closed the door, got dressed and went back to the Forward Command Post. There were still a few AFP and INP judiciously working away processing Salik's and Misno's items. I logged into my computer and entered the phone number into the database. Out of the approximate 26,000 entries in the electronic investigation file – nothing. *Fuck, I'll deal with this in the morning*, I thought as I logged off.

I now had even more questions rattling in my mind. *Who was he and how did he know which room was mine? Why did he want to give me a phone number and why give it to me in the middle of the night?*

As I was walking back to my room, I weighed up what I knew of the encounter. He was Indonesian. He gave me a bum

LONG SHOTS

Indonesian phone number. Hundreds of people knew the AFP had a 24-hour Forward Command Post in the president's suite of the Kartika Plaza, yet he came to my room specifically; he clearly wanted to give me the number directly. He didn't want Detachment 88 to know about it. Was he just some random lunatic or was there more to it?

Then it dawned on me. He had to be from BIN. He wanted to assist with the investigation, but he didn't want INP to get any credit. If this was true, then it couldn't be a bum phone number. There had to be more to it.

The following morning, I met Sam for breakfast.

'Mate this one's just between you and I. Can you work on this phone number but don't tell anyone else please?'

'That's all very secret squirrel. Where'd the number come from?'

'Can't say, just see what you can find out about it. It might be a good one or it might be a total furphy.'

During the morning, I felt guilty talking with Gilang and Harta about the investigation and not sharing the new information I had. However, as I didn't know who gave me the information, I needed to play by the rules so I wouldn't ruin any chance of him coming back to me, hopefully with better information. About 10 am, Sam asked if I wanted to go for a coffee, indicating he had something to tell me. We walked outside to one of the beachfront cafes and sat at a table away from others.

'Where did you get that number from, Ice?'

'Like I said, mate, I can't say. What'd you find out?'

'It's a legitimate Indonesian phone number. It's been connected for about ten weeks. The SIM card was bought from Surabaya.'

'Is it active now?'

'It's still connected. It's being turned on for a couple of minutes every few days. Looking at the history of pings, it's never been to Bali. Last location was Malang. I know what you're going to say, about a million people live there.'

'I'm happy with one in a million odds right now, there's nothing wrong with taking long shots.'

'It's not that bad. Here's the good oil. I put the phone number in the database and it's one of the 20 or so numbers INP found written on a page in Misno's house,' Sam said, trying to control his excitement.

'But I'd already run the number last night, and it drew a blank.'

'The last of the property was only entered in the database this morning, so perhaps it wasn't there when you searched,' Sam said.

'We can't sit on this information. We need to get a phone intercept. I'll have a talk with Gilang.'

Knowing the only way we could get a phone intercept was via the INP, I asked Gilang if he would come for a walk. On a number of occasions when we had something very sensitive to discuss, we would do it walking around the lush gardens surrounding the Kartika Plaza. So my invite was intriguing but not surprising.

We walked along the beachfront watching ancient Balinese women giving massages on cane mats while bright-eyed teenagers hawked fake brand T-shirts and sunglasses to unsuspecting tourists. 'Gilang, I can't tell you where I got the information from but one of the phone numbers found in Misno's house looks very suspicious.'

'Ah, from Australian intelligence hey Dave,' he said, giving me a knowing wink.

Seizing on the loophole Gilang created I replied, 'Well, you know, mate, we can't discuss any of this officially.'

'Of course,' he agreed.

Within hours Detachment 88 had a live intercept on the phone number – we just needed the phone to be turned on so we could locate it. For security, the INP field phone intercept team, who was already monitoring a number of other phones, was working at a secret location not far from the Kartika Plaza.

Criminals rarely abide by the script written for television so, while this was an interesting development, if the phone was ever turned on again, it was expected to take days, if not weeks. So, in the meantime, everyone in the Forward Command Post continued with several other lines of enquiry.

DEFEATING TERROR

Late that afternoon I asked Harta if he would like to meet for dinner. 'Yes, of course, Dave. I'm still fasting for Ramadan, so as long as it's after sunset I would love to.' he replied.

Most of the INP in the Forward Command Post were Muslim, so I was well aware of the fasting obligations they had until Friday 4 November 2005, when Eid al-Fitr (Celebration of the Breaking of the Fast) would commence. The Eid al-Fitr celebrations are a major event in the Muslim calendar, celebrated similarly to the Christmas holidays in Western countries. Until the end of Ramadan, out of fairness and respect for our Muslim colleagues, AFP staff in the Forward Command Post were discreet when it came to drinking, eating and smoking during the daylight hours.

During dinner that night, it was brought home to me that my obsessive dedication to find the terrorists was matched by Harta and most of his Muslim colleagues when I asked, 'So, Eid is the day after tomorrow, will you be going back to see your family over the break?'

'Some have decided to take a couple of days off, but most of us will stay here and keep working.'

'You really are mad.'

'Yeah, I know. That's what my wife said when I told her I wouldn't be coming home,' Harta confessed.

'Mind you if it was the Christmas break, I'd stay here too ... and my wife would say the same thing to me.'

LONG SHOTS

We gave each other a smile and he said, 'Who'd be a police officer?'

Two days later, the Eid al-Fitr celebrations commenced. On the first day of the celebrations in his Batu hideout, Azhari, assisted by Cholili and Arman, peeled the newspaper off the windows of their dingy mountainside villa. They opened the windows and doors and allowed the fresh mountain air to replace the dankness ... and the smell of explosives.

Then, under the guise of celebrating Eid al-Fitr, for the first time they spoke to their neighbours. The trio invited several of them in for the pastries and tea they had prepared. Neighbours would later tell me they saw university textbooks and laptops. This aligned with the cover story they had been told, that the three men were going to Malang University. What none of them noticed was that one door of the three-bedroom house remained locked. That room was chock-a-block with evidence of their real intent. Another neighbour told me that during their 'open house' day, Azhari played games with a young boy who lived across the road, probably because he missed his son who was in Malaysia. Azhari's rat-cunning plan allayed any fears in the village that the occupants of the villa were anything but genuine university students.

Five days later, at about 5 am on 9 November, I was once again woken by a soft knock at the door. This time my head switched on a lot faster and I was prepared to grill the mystery man for more information. However, as I opened the door I saw Harta's familiar smile and gleaming gold tooth. 'Dave, you've gotta come into the FCP, we have something good.'

I hurriedly pulled on a pair of board shorts and a singlet and scuffed my thongs along the tiled hallway in pursuit of Harta. We entered the Forward Command Post and I was surprised to see so many INP officers packing bags and gathering equipment.

With his usual quiet demeanour Harta said, 'This is a message that was just texted to the Misno number, about an hour ago,' as he handed me a piece of paper with the English translation: *T wants cake. Semarang.*

'T! That's gotta be Top!' I said.

'Yes, that's what we think too. We've captured the number that sent the text, but it's turned off at the moment so we don't have a location. But the Misno number is still turned on. It's currently outside Surabaya and by the pings it's heading slowly towards Semarang,' Harta said.

'How long would it take someone to drive from Surabaya to Semarang?' I asked.

'About three hours. We're flying straight to Semarang at 6.30, so we'll get there at least an hour before the earliest arrival time. The only question is, where is he going to meet Top? It's a big city, there's over one million people in Semarang.'

'We're always pushing against the odds aren't we?' I mumbled.

LONG SHOTS

'Yeah. Gilang's already at the airport, are you coming with us, brother?' Harta said with a smile betraying his understated personality.

The AFP in Indonesia don't have any legal police powers, don't carry weapons and are instructed to avoid situations such as this. So, it was an offer I had to decline. 'No mate. I'd love to, but I'd be more use back here. I'll assign a couple of agents and an interpreter and lock them away with your tracking team to help monitor the phone live. That way we can keep you and Gilang updated.'

Then I paused as the reality of what might happen sank in. 'Harta, be careful out there, mate. You know this bloke carries a bomb, he's fucken mad.'

With that Harta slapped my shoulder, flashed me a smile and then slung a heavy duffel bag over his shoulder and made for the door, followed by a conga line of eager INP. The familiar *clank* of guns and magazines echoed from inside their luggage as they walked down the long corridor.

They had a date with a terrorist. Lucky bastards.

BATU SILENCE

By 6 am, Sam and two others were assisting the INP with tracking the Misno phone as it slowly made its way closer to Semarang. This was prior to smart phones with GPS so, unlike in spy movies, we couldn't accurately pinpoint the phone's location. The location algorithm targeting the phone at best could narrow it down to about a 100-metre radius. That's very useful in a rural area where there aren't many people, but we knew whoever had the bomb for 'T' was headed for Semarang. So our goal was to identify the person before he reached the densely populated area where it would be impossible to isolate the phone.

Over the next few hours, frantic INP surveillance vehicles were racing along the 300 kilometres of fragmented Jalan Pantura highway trying to marry up the pings with traffic moving along the highway. Not a needle in a haystack, but not far from it either.

Travelling among the many vehicles on the highway

BATU SILENCE

towards Semarang that day was Cholili on his motorcycle. In his backpack was a modular bomb, one of many that he and Azhari had assembled since the Bali attack. Around his waist was a bum bag bomb, primed and ready to detonate.

About an hour out of Semarang, he pulled over to the side of the road near a rice paddy. His location was immediately relayed to the field surveillance team. This was a perfect place to isolate the phone from the moving traffic. Unfortunately, none of the surveillance vehicles were close to his location at that stage. Cholili would have propped the bike on its kickstand and raised the hinged dark visor on his helmet revealing his face – another missed opportunity. From the phone tracking room in Bali, INP officers were giving urgent updates to the surveillance team who were racing towards the stationary ping.

Cholili stood beside the road, giving his legs a much-needed stretch while he took in the vista of the majestic mountain range surrounding the rice fields. Most likely enjoying the break with a freshly lit cigarette protruding from his thin lips, he fished around in the backpack for his phone. He wanted to turn it on so he could receive a text from 'T' identifying where in Semarang they would meet. As he retrieved the phone from within the darkness of the bag, he must have immediately noticed the blue light emanating from its screen and realised he'd left it turned on after receiving the last text. It was a careless mistake that breached one of the most important security measures drilled into him by Azhari.

A call came into the phone tracking room from the Indonesian surveillance team leader on the road. 'We've just gone through the turnoff to Demak, how far away is he?'

'About 10 kilometres,' the tracking officer replied.

Then the ping on the tracking laptop disappeared. The phone had been turned off.

'He's turned the phone off!' the tracking officer yelled into the phone.

'Shit,' said the surveillance team leader as he pressed the odometer reset button, planted his foot even harder on the accelerator and watched as the dials turned over towards 10 kilometres.

Totally unaware and probably feeling better after the nicotine hit and leg stretch, Cholili kickstarted the motorcycle and re-joined the traffic. In the tracking room, enthusiasm and excitement were replaced with silence as we watched the screen hopefully. Nothing.

Then one of the Indonesian tracking officers' phones rang. The call was from the central telephone intercept monitoring room in Jakarta. 'Just before the phone was turned off, a text was sent from it,' the phone's speaker echoed.

'What? What did it say?' the tracking officer asked.

'"Bus", that's all. Just the word "Bus."'

BATU SILENCE

'Okay, we'll keep watching from here. Let us know if any other messages or phone calls are made,' then the officer hung up and immediately called Gilang.

'Sir, a text was just sent with just the word "Bus". He must be meeting someone arriving on a bus.'

'Thanks, I'll call you back,' came Gilang's succinct reply.

Gilang and the others, who had arrived from Bali about an hour earlier, covertly infiltrated the crowded Semarang bus terminal. Each man knew exactly what Top looked like and secretly scanned every arriving bus passenger.

Then, one of the team rang Gilang: 'I've just seen Cholili. I'm sure it's him.'

'Really. Where is he?' Gilang asked as his mind ran through the vast number of persons of interest. Cholili was one, but he was just a minor player.

'He's sitting on a motorcycle parked next to the fountain outside the bus station. He's just sitting there smoking.'

'That's one heck of a coincidence. He must be here to meet Top,' concluded Gilang. 'Well I'd like to have a talk with him. Take two others with you and ask him what he's doing here, but keep it low key. I don't want to spook Top.'

A short time later three covert INP officers discreetly converged on Cholili. 'Hey,' one of the officers said, expecting to have a conversation. Immediately Cholili sprang to his feet, surprising the officers.

'Get back! I've got a bomb!'

The officers immediately recoiled and drew their firearms.

'I mean it, get back!' Cholili screamed.

'Okay, take it easy,' said one of the officers as he re-holstered his pistol. As soon as the firearm was secured, the officer courageously dived at Cholili's waist, tackling him to the ground. Cholili had his hand on the detonation switch – but didn't activate it.

'Okay, okay, stop. Don't hurt me,' he squealed.

The ruckus drew the attention of the remaining INP officers who were inside the terminal waiting for Top. Several of them ran out to assist with Cholili's now very public arrest. As this occurred Teddy arrived on a motor scooter with Anif as his passenger. Teddy, thinking that the police were on to all of them, immediately pulled out a handgun and fired two shots at police before accelerating away. The acceleration caught Anif by surprise and he fell backwards off the motorcycle, landing heavily on the road. As he attempted to get up, police pounced and pinned him to the ground. Teddy sped off into the obscurity of the fast-flowing traffic.

Detachment 88 officers whisked Cholili and Anif off to a Semarang safe house to be interviewed rather than to the local police station where word of their arrests might be leaked by police sympathetic to JI. Anif made some minor admissions to his involvement with the Bali attacks, but that was all. Cholili,

BATU SILENCE

though, couldn't talk fast enough as he attempted to save himself. He immediately told police that Azhari was staying in a villa in Batu, Malang with a person he knew as Arman. He also explained that he and Teddy were working as the middlemen between Azhari and Top and that 'T' in the text messages stood for Teddy, not Top.

Our mistake was later leaked in a confidential US cable, that stated:

> They all point to heavy involvement by a fugitive named Tedy/Teddy alias Reno. Initially, both the INP and the Australian Federal Police believed 'Tedy' to be an alias of Noordin Mohommad [*sic*] Top, but they now know Tedy exists.[121]

Unfortunately for police, Cholili didn't know where Top's hideout was, but he knew precisely where his housemate, Azhari, lived. As far as the police were concerned, this information was as good as it gets. They didn't want to miss Azhari again, so the Detachment 88 officers worked quickly. By 1 pm that afternoon, with the assistance of the heavily armed Brimob (SWAT), Detachment 88 had silently surrounded Azhari's villa.

Isolated from the rapid chain of events, and still thinking we had lost contact with the Misno number, I had remained

225

DEFEATING TERROR

in the tracking room with other disillusioned police. Just after 2 pm, my phone rang. It was a very excited Gilang.

'Dave, we are about to pounce. We have Azhari surrounded in Batu. This is it! I've gotta go.'

'How did you—', I started to ask.

I stood there stunned for a moment. While Azhari and Top had always been the primary suspects, just two hours before we were tracking the Misno phone *hoping* whoever had it was meeting with Top. Now they had Azhari's house surrounded? I had no idea that Anif and Cholili had been arrested and that this had revealed Azhari's current location. I told the other tracking officers what was about to happen in Batu. Anticipation flooded the room, but no-one was game to celebrate.

From behind the concrete fence of a property about 100 metres from Azhari's villa, Gilang shattered the Batu silence as he squeezed the trigger on the loud hailer.

'Azhari Husin. This is superintendent Gilang Herianto. You are surrounded. You and anyone else in there need to come out with your hands up. Now!'

Gilang's tinny-sounding, amplified command reverberated between the villas down the narrow street and slowly faded away. Then a single gunshot cracked from the house. Its projectile parted the tensed flesh of a Brimob officer's thigh before striking the bone, crippling him. Before he had hit the

BATU SILENCE

ground, Indonesian police returned with incredible firepower from all directions, shattering the windows and punctuating the exterior cement walls with bullet hail-marks. After the intense volley, silence again returned.

'Azhari, can you hear me?' blasted the loud hailer.

'Yes, I can hear you. No more shooting, I've been hurt. I can't get up,' screamed Azhari from somewhere inside the villa.

'Is anyone else in there with you?'

'No. I'm by myself,' came the feeble reply.

Gilang looked to the Brimob team leader, who with a silent nod gestured to a group of his men. Robotically, the men in black overalls with machine guns pressed firmly to their shoulders tactically moved in-turn towards the house. From neighbouring rooftops Brimob snipers took up positions to cover their colleagues. Just 30 metres from the house, the advancing team took cover, propping behind power poles, cement fences and vehicles.

'Azhari, you have to open the front door,' Gilang demanded.

'I can't. I can't move.'

In unison, the advance team stood up with their weapons trained on the house and slowly but surely progressed forwards. The team leader paused near the concrete side fence and gestured to the rest of the team to halt. Suddenly, a plastic Tupperware container was thrown through the shredded curtain of the front window, landing on the ground next to the fence. The team

DEFEATING TERROR

leader dived for cover as the container exploded its hellfire of white-hot ball bearings.

Immediately a rain of fire from the snipers poured in through the villa windows. Arman lay prone on the floor unharmed, but frozen by fear as the bullets peppered the floor around him. Sheltering under a front window, Azhari primed another bomb and, during a pause in the gunfire, he threw it with all his strength towards the police, now cowering behind fences and vehicles just metres away. The deadly explosion sent a shockwave through their bodies, but none of the shrapnel hit their mark.

In response, Gilang, Harta and the rest of the Detachment 88 officers fired their weapons from every quarter. Uninjured, Azhari primed another bomb and threw it through the window onto the street, sending shrapnel ricocheting in all directions. Again, the steel hail missed the Brimob officers who remained pinned in their cover positions. It was only a matter of time until Azhari would find his range, so using hand signals the Brimob team leader then directed his team to withdraw.

In support of their trapped colleagues, the surrounding Detachment 88 officers poured deadly fire into the building, allowing the Brimob officers to retreat to safer positions – shaken but unharmed by their brush with death.

No sooner had the covering police fire paused than the intervening silence was shattered with another explosive device thrown from the house. Instantly, the police replied with more gunfire. This sequence was repeated like a deadly tennis match volleying bombs and gunfire for the next 30 minutes, until Gilang ordered the police to stop shooting.

Seizing on the lull, with an apparently very shaky wrist, Arman let fly several indiscriminate shots from his revolver. This was quickly answered by the police, who only stopped firing when Gilang raised his loud hailer.

'Azhari come out now with your hands up. Now! Quickly!' Gilang yelled.

'Why don't you come in and arrest me,' taunted Azhari.

Not taking the wannabe martyr's bait, Gilang commanded, 'Come out now. There's no escape for you.'

Arman, having reloaded the pistol, raised his hand and fired again. This was immediately answered with an enfilade of police fire showering through the windows and into the external walls of the building.

From crime scene analysis, it appears Azhari then slid a suicide vest across the hallway to Arman. Azhari slithered into his own vest and must have seen Arman was struggling to fit the device. Considering the police had failed to take the bait and come into the house, it's likely at this stage that Azhari was planning for himself and Arman to charge at the police and detonate themselves within killing range of their enemy.

DEFEATING TERROR

Apparently seeing Arman's difficulty, Azhari sprang from his firing position and sprinted across the room and into the crosshairs of a Brimob sniper who fired into Azhari's chest, felling him.

Stunned, Arman must have struggled but eventually pulled the vest on as he watched in horror while Azhari writhed on the floor like an injured snake, smearing claret across the tiles. Perhaps encouraged by Azhari, or motivated by his own wish to die as a martyr, Arman crouched in position and readied himself for his death sprint for Allah.

Arman's vest was fitted with two switches, the right switch for immediate detonation and the left switch for a delay detonation – perfect for activating before running at the police. When there was a break in the gunfire, Arman pressed the left (delay detonation) switch downwards, but in doing so his shaking hand also simultaneously pressed the right switch.

Electrons instantaneously flowed from the 9-volt battery through the circuitry, detonating the explosive packages. Arman's torso was immediately liquefied and sprayed mist-like through the room. Streaming through the crimson cloud, sparks of ball-bearing shrapnel vectored outwards with fatal force, shredding Azhari's flesh. The fiery fist of the blast punched Azhari's ragdoll body across the floor, collapsing the kitchen wall on top of him. There he died, his body riddled with ball bearings, a victim of his own infernal designs.

BATU SILENCE

A large cloud of acrid smoke billowed from the villa and plumed into the air. The front wall of the villa had been blown out and the rubble had cascaded onto the street. Finally, after hundreds of rounds had been fired and 11 bombs had been detonated, the Batu silence returned.

Cautiously, the police closed in. Among the dusty bloody brick mess, they found Azhari's laptop with several new terrorist plots saved on the hard drive, and his personal diary, containing two handwritten letters in Malay.

One was a letter, not yet posted, to Nur Aini, which stated,

To die in such a way will assure me a place in heaven and enable me to bring 70 members of our extended family. Remember me to our son and take care of him.

The other letter was *from* Nur Aini, expressing her fears that he may be killed and informing him that their son, 'frequently uttered the word "grave" in his sleep'.[122]

Terror touches everyone.

A MUSLIM AND TWO CHRISTIANS WALK INTO A BAR

That night the news of Azhari's death made headlines around the world, with video of the shootout leading most news reports. The stories blared the heroic and dedicated efforts of the INP. They deserved it.

The following day I asked Ketut to drive to the airport so I could catch a flight to Surabaya. He seemed subdued as we snaked our way through the morning traffic. His normal chirpy banter was absent and he was more focused on the road than making jokes. Wanting to lighten the mood a little, I said, 'Everything ok, mate? You seem quiet.'

'Yes,' came the curt reply.

The trip continued with unusual quiet all the way to Denpasar Airport where he pulled the Tarago to a jolt in the drop-off zone. Usually Ketut would spring from his seat and assist with unloading luggage. Not this time.

After grabbing my bags, I walked to the driver's window. 'Well, Ketut, I won't be flying back to Bali, so I won't see you again. Thanks for all your help over the past few weeks. I really appreciate it.'

Ketut focused straight ahead and mumbled, 'You shouldn't have shared that phone number.'

'What?' I asked, surprised by the comment.

Maintaining his focus, Ketut said, 'We trusted you.'

Before I could say anything, he dropped the clutch and accelerated away. As I stood there in the blue cloud of exhaust smoke, I wondered who Ketut really was. Was he an Azhari supporter who was angered by his death? Did he work for BIN? Did he work for some other foreign organisation? Perhaps he was just a *bemo* driver – but I doubted it.

Puzzled, looking over my shoulder more than usual and eager to be in the company of Gilang and Harta, who I trusted would provide me protection if necessary, I flew direct to Surabaya. There I spent many hours interviewing Cholili and some other JI radicals. Cholili was a quietly spoken, polite and pleasant-looking man, as were the others.

During the interviews, it was hard for me to fathom the immense level of hatred these men had in the name of their religion. They hated me and everything I stood for before they had even met me. They didn't know my religion, and it didn't matter. I wasn't Muslim, therefore they had an obligation to hate me. These misguided Muslims believe there is a holy war being fought between Islam and Christians, Jews, Hindus, Buddhists, agnostics and atheists – everyone. Success in the war will only be reached when the entire world is Islamic and abides by Sharia law. They were, in the purest sense, Islamofascists forcing their agenda on the world, akin to the Nazis.

The views of these men were starkly conflicted by those of Harta and the other Muslim police officers I worked with during that investigation and others. They believed in democracy and the rule of law and didn't have hatred for others at the core of their existence. They were just like me and most other Australians with diverse religious views.

On my last night in Indonesia, Gilang and Harta took me out for dinner. Afterwards we went to a quiet bar in the hotel where we sat at a secluded corner table. The pleasant waitress arrived with a soft drink for Harta and beers for Gilang and myself.

'So, I hope I never have to work with either of you two again. That'd mean that there's been another anthrax or bomb attack,' I said lightheartedly.

Gilang burst out with laughter. 'Don't go setting off any bombs just to get us together again.'

A MUSLIM AND TWO CHRISTIANS WALK INTO A BAR

Harta's gentle smile appeared. 'No more bombs. Shit, I've seen enough. I think I need a quiet desk job now.'

'You'd get bored after a week and want to be back in the field chasing terrorists,' I teased.

With his broadening smile revealing his gold tooth, Harta said, 'You're probably right Dave. *Allahu Akbar!*' He raised his drink.

Gilang and I raised our glasses and the three vessels clinked at the centre of the table as I said, 'You're right, mate, God is great.'[123]

AFTERMATH

On 11 November 2005, two days after the shootout, AFP Commissioner Mick Keelty, talking to ABC radio from Thailand, stated that

> hand-picked [Australian] federal police officers were a core element in the joint tracking team that picked up Azhari's trail a few days ago and finally pinned him down to a hideout in the Javanese resort town of Batu.[124]

Keelty also stated, 'Australian police have been helping the Indonesians track Azhari since the first Bali bombing and had a team close to the scene of the shootout that ended in his death.'[125]

Media reported also that there were nine permanently attached AFP officers in Jakarta and Bali and about 25 to 30 'in the field' depending on operational needs. This offered, for the very first time, a very public glimpse into the secretive work the AFP were doing by taking the fight to terrorists offshore. A fight that continues today.

AFTERMATH

On 18 November 2005, farewell videos by Ayip Hidayat, Salik Firdaus and Misno were made public on a JI website. A fourth video was also released which showed Top, dressed in a balaclava, threatening Western countries and specifically urging strikes against Australia.[126]

On 7 June 2006, the first trials for the 1 October 2005 Bali bombings commenced. The defendants were Mohammad Cholili and Anif Solchanudin, and Dwi Widiyarto[127] and Abdul Aziz,[128] who created the website and published the videos. Each man was charged under Indonesian articles 6 and 15 of the 2003 Anti-Terrorism Law for participating in terrorist activities, carrying a maximum penalty of death.

In September 2006, Mohammad Cholili was sentenced to 18 years. He served less than eight years and was released in August 2014.

In September 2006, Anif Solchanudin was sentenced to 15 years. He served less than half of that. In 2014, he was filmed in a pro-ISIS video filmed at a mosque in Solo, Central Java.

In September 2006, Abdul Aziz and Dwi Widiyarto were each sentenced to eight years for assisting Top and for publishing Top's video and that of the three suicide bombers. The site also provided instructions on how to kill non-Muslims in Jakarta.

On 8 November 2008, Mukhlas was executed for his role in the Bali One bombing.

DEFEATING TERROR

On 9 November 2008, Amrozi and Imam Samudra were executed for their roles in the Bali One bombing. Ali Imron was convicted for his role in the Bali One bombing and was sentenced to life imprisonment.

In September 2009, Noor Din bin Mohammed Top was killed by Detachment 88 officers during a raid in Semarang.

In 2009, Idris was released after serving five years of his 10-year sentence for the JW Marriott Hotel bombing. He confessed to involvement with the Bali One bombing and to personally detonating the motorcycle bomb near the US consulate, but was acquitted on appeal before Indonesia's constitutional court that held that retrospective terror laws (introduced after the Bali One bombing) were unconstitutional.

On 9 March 2010, Dulmatin was killed by Detachment 88 officers during a raid in Jakarta.

In 2004, Abu Bakar Bashir was arrested for conspiracy in relation to the Bali One bombing. In 2006, he had his conviction overturned. In 2011, he was sentenced to 15 years' imprisonment for financial involvement with a terror training camp in Aceh. On 5 August 2016, he failed in a bid to have this conviction overturned.

On 22 September 2016, Indonesian authorities intercepted a vessel illegally importing 30 tonnes of ammonium nitrate. The vessel had left from Malaysia and was bound for Bali.

EVER

I knew that during the process of writing this book I would need to return to Indonesia to conduct additional interviews and source new information.[129] I had not been back since the Bali Two investigation in 2005, which had altered my fun-filled perception of the country, specifically of Bali.

I also knew that I would need to travel into parts of Java where JI remains active, places where I would not be welcome – in fact, I would be hated. Not just for being white, Australian or a Westerner, but if it were revealed that I had been a senior AFP officer, I would be a prime target. As one of those at the centre of tracking down and killing Azhari, one of the organisation's heroes, there would be legitimate religious value on my head – literally. They could have easily justified their barbaric act 'defending Islam' by quoting the Koran:

When you meet the unbelievers strike off their heads and, when you have wreaked widespread slaughter among them, bind your captives firmly. Then either grant them their freedom or take a ransom from them, until war shall lay down her burdens. Thus shall you do.[130]

The problem is not the Koran; other religious texts, including the Bible, also contain equally violent passages. The danger arises when fanatics choose selected ancient edicts such as this as justification for modern-day violence. Unless you are a strict Muslim, they could apply this Sharia command to you too; and if you think having no religious belief will save you, think again. Being an atheist is worse than being a Christian – at least Muslims and Christians share a belief in Jesus.[131] There is no get-out-of-jail-free card for anyone who does not share their worldview, including the 'wrong sort' of Muslims.

I had no intention of starring in the next beheading video on YouTube, so venturing into these parts was a carefully considered and calculated risk. I'd been trained in international covert operations and had spent a year in Afghanistan with NATO, so I wasn't new to such a deployment. However, considering the potential risks, it was still one I'd rather not do alone. I knew Sam had recently retired from the AFP and he was familiar with these areas, having worked in Southeast Asian terror tracking teams for several years. So, I made a phone call and explained the task and the locations to him.

EVER

'Really, Ice? I've just retired. The last time I was in those places I had a team of Detachment 88 blokes with machine guns for protection. It's pretty hostile territory. You sure you want go there?' he said.

'Yeah. It's just one last deployment, mate. It'll be a walk in the park,' I said sarcastically.

'Alright,' he replied with his deadpan tone – he could never walk away from a challenge.

We then carefully planned the trip using our best tradecraft techniques to mitigate as much risk as possible. Weeks later we were in the heart of it. While there, one of the places I wanted to visit was the site where Azhari was killed in the Batu shootout. Not to celebrate his death or to revel in a professional success; while it was tempting to dance on his death site and sing a song of vengeance on behalf of all those he killed and injured, that wasn't my purpose. I'm not a victim of Azhari's evil, so I would never be as presumptuous as to forgive him on behalf of those who endured the horror he delivered. However, I wanted to acknowledge him as a human being whose life had been wasted in the pointless pursuit of Islamic terrorism.

Today, Raja's and the Menega Cafe and Nyoman restaurants continue to be full of foreign tourists enjoying Bali – in 2017, I was one of them. Other nightclubs and bars are again packed with people enjoying freedom of, and freedom from, religion.

With the grim exception of the bombing victims and their grieving families, and increased economic hardship for some Balinese businesses, nothing has changed. Azhari's life mission was pointless.

There had been a time when he was a balanced-minded Muslim. He'd been an exemplary university student, a respected academic and, according to Nur Aini, at some stage a good husband and father. As a student in Adelaide he'd been, 'a good guy' who was quick to make people laugh.[132] I've lived in Adelaide and spent considerable time studying at universities. We could have met as colleagues on a university campus. He could have even become a friend. But his extreme religious choice set him on a path at odds with the vast majority of Muslims, and the rest of the world.

Azhari left his cancer-afflicted wife and two children destitute, pursuing his perverted quest to right the world by killing innocent people he had never met. Believing Allah would view him favourably if he died as a martyr, he was never going to surrender to the police. They made the correct decision that day in Batu.

I do not hate Muslims. I hate terrorists. Considering the circumstances, I too would have pulled the trigger that day in Batu — not because of his religion, but because he was a dangerous criminal. Azhari's death was unfortunate, but necessary, for the sake of those he was still planning to kill.

EVER

Now, in 2017, it wouldn't have furthered the cause of justice, humanity or healing for me to debauch his death site. Instead, I placed a palm frond (a Sunni Muslim tradition) on his death site, to acknowledge the passing of another human being: a man who had been diverted from decency by intolerant and inflexible Islamic beliefs. Beliefs that are completely incompatible with cultural and religious diversity, equality and democracy.

JI has been decimated over the past few years, thanks largely to the Indonesian police. However, there is still no shortage of JI members and their network still exists today. There are also several other radicalised Islamic groups in Indonesia. They continue to pose a danger to those they consider their enemies. As I travelled through JI's Javanese heartland, I knew there were some in the surrounding communities that would have taken great delight in beheading me (as they would you), purely because I was culturally and religiously different from them.

Cowardly Islamic beheadings are not confined to Asia or the Middle East; they've also been conducted in the UK and Europe. Australia is not immune from this barbarity. In 2016, Sevdet Ramadan Besam pleaded guilty in a Melbourne court to one charge of planning a terrorist act. He had planned to drive over and then behead a police officer at an Anzac Day parade to, in his words, 'make sure the dogs remember this as well as their fallen heroes'. [133]

DEFEATING TERROR

On 18 April 2015, less than five hours after typing into his phone the reasons why he intended to undertake the attack and how he wanted his burial dealt with and his possessions dispersed after his death, Besam was arrested: an outstanding example of the vigilance and cooperation of the AFP and its partners. Besam joins a list of more than 20 people convicted 'beyond reasonable doubt' in Australian courts for terrorist offences. But for the continued dedication of the men and women of the AFP, the Australian intelligence community and the state and territory police to protecting lives, Australia's terrorism death toll would be much higher.

Members of the public are an incredibly vital source of information for these organisations. I am aware of cases where terrorists were in the advanced stages of planning an attack and if it wasn't for a tipoff from a member of the public, the attack would most likely have been successful; deaths and injury would have resulted.

In the event of an unexpected attack, people are sometimes very quick to point a finger at law enforcement's 'failure' to prevent it. This is unfair, unrealistic and hurtful to the vigilant men and women who work every day to try to prevent such attacks. An unexpected terrorist attack is a community failure; someone always knows something about an attack before it happens. You either support terrorism or you act against it. There is no excuse for anyone under

EVER

any circumstances to withhold anything that may prevent indiscriminate murder.

The question: what kind of teachings can rationalise such hatred? Azhari had been inspired by Islamic leaders who knew better and had been assisted by Muslim community members who remained silent. Either group could have put a stop to his rampage before it started. This would have saved lives and better promoted the reputation of Islam and what it really means to be Muslim.

Understanding any religion, or the lack thereof, is a minefield of interpretation. I've read as much of the Koran as I have of the Bible and I've also spent some time reading about other religions. It seems there's a multitude of interpretations within every area of spiritual belief. I don't for a moment profess to understand any religion comprehensively.

But it's a simple task of looking to the fruits borne by a particular religion; that's how to judge its value. If it produces overt acts of peace, tolerance and goodwill to others, including those of other religions, then that belief system is fine by me. To each their own.

To make it abundantly clear, I am *not* in any way criticising Islam; most Muslims are good people and a vital part of our diverse society. It's those who misuse religion to validate violence I have a problem with, regardless of whether they are Christian, Muslim, Jewish, Hindu, Buddhist or another faith.

DEFEATING TERROR

Since 2000, more than 17,000 people have been killed in Islamic conflicts and more than 42,000 injured — and the majority of these victims are law-abiding, peaceful Muslims caught in the crossfire of perceived religious wars.[134]

A Moroccan academic who spent more than 20 years studying Islam, and whose father was an imam, stated,

> ISIL, Al Qaeda, Boko Haram, al-Shabaab in Somalia, the Taliban and their sister brand names are all made in Islam. Unless the Muslim world deals with Islam and separates religion from state, we will never end this cycle [of violence].[135]

The heavy lifting out of this violent religious quagmire needs to be led by strong Muslim communities, promoting twenty-first-century values, particularly through moderate youth education. Additionally, it seems clear that reformation, and increased denunciation of terrorism by Muslim authorities needs to be amplified. For this to occur, the Muslim community need to be confident they are standing on the shoulders of the broader multidenominational community. Everyone, particularly those who denounce terrorism and act against it, deserves our support.

Some have suggested using immigration policies to ban all Muslims. This isn't the answer; it's simply ridiculous. Islamic

EVER

terrorists are the problem – not Muslims. Islamophobia is just as poisonous as Islamofacism – both are fuelled by ignorance and hate. Freedom of religion is a human right: every person is entitled to exercise it, if they so choose. Theological difference should not create division or animosity, but should be harnessed and promoted. A promising example of this recently occurred in Beaconsfield, Western Australia. Imam Feizel Chothia informed Anglican Reverend Peter Humphris that he was looking for a place for Muslims to pray. Reverend Humphris opened the doors to his Christian church and the community hall.

Now Muslim community members pray and share the same church precinct with Christians. Reverend Humphris said, 'My prayer is that there will always be a diversity of religions ... that we will honour each other and discover that it's in that diversity that we've got life.'

Imam Feizel Chothia also supported religious diversity, saying:

> The Prophet [Muhammad] interestingly says, the difference of opinion is the source of the greatest blessing because your ideas and your preconceived notions or orthodoxies are challenged ... the Prophet gave Christians sanctuary for prayers at his mosque in Medina, Saudi Arabia in the seventh century.'[136]

DEFEATING TERROR

The two communities are now planning to build a water feature for Christian rituals and Muslim ablutions – together. Terrorism is a together problem; together we face the same threats, and only together will they be mitigated. We live on a big planet, and there's room for all religions – but there is no room for religious violence. Ever.

MAIN PLAYERS

Abu Bakar Bashir (Bashir): Born 17 August 1938 in Jombang Regency, Indonesia but of Yemeni descent. Cofounder of JI with Sungkar. In 1973 he cofounded with Sungkar the infamously radicalising institution for children, the Al-Mukmin *pesantren* (Islamic boarding school) in Ngruki on the eastern suburbs of Solo. In 2004, Abu Bakar Bashir was arrested for conspiracy in relation to the Bali One bombing. In 2006, he had his conviction for involvement in that bombing overturned. In 2011, he was sentenced to 15 years imprisonment for financial involvement with a terror training camp in Aceh. On 5 August 2016, he failed in a bid to have his conviction overturned and remains in jail. He denies JI exists and that it has been made up by Western government agencies, including the CIA, to discredit Muslims.

Abdullah Achmad bin Sungkar (Sungkar): Born on an unknown date in 1937 in Solo, Central Java, Indonesia. Cofounder of JI with Bashir. Cofounder with Bashir of the infamously

DEFEATING TERROR

radicalising institution for children, the Al–Mukmin *pesantren* (Islamic boarding school). Died of a heart attack in 1999.

Hambali: Born 4 April 1964, Cianjur, West Java, Indonesia. Real name Nurjaman bin Isamuddin, Hambali was also known as Riduan Isamuddin and Encep. In 1985, he was radicalised by Sungkar in Malaysia. Hambali, sometimes referred to as the Osama bin Laden of Southeast Asia, was the linchpin between JI and Al–Qaeda. On 11 August 2003, he and his Malaysian wife were arrested in Ayutthaya (70 kilometres outside Bangkok), Thailand. Involved with planning for the bombing of the USS *Cole*, 9/11, the Bali One bombing, the Marriott hotel bombing, the Indonesian Christmas Eve church attacks and the aborted Singapore attack plan. Believed to be still detained at Guantanamo Bay, Cuba.

Azhari bin Husin (Azhari): Born on 14 September 1957 in Malacca, 150 kilometres south of Kuala Lumpur, Malaysia. He is sometimes referred to as Azahari. Failed university in South Australia in the 1980s. Graduate degree completed in Malaysia. PhD in statistical modelling attained at Reading University, UK. Married Wan Nur Aini Jusoh (Nur Aini) in Johor, Malaysia in November 1985. Father of two children with Nur Aini, a daughter, Aisyah, and son, Zaid Abil. Radicalised predominantly by Sungkar and Bashir. Became JI's master

MAIN PLAYERS

bomb-maker. Directly involved with the Indonesian Christmas Eve church attacks, bombings of Bali One, the Marriott hotel, the Australian embassy Jakarta, Bali Two and planning the aborted Singapore attack plan. Killed in a shootout with police in Batu, Malang, East Java on 9 November 2005.

Mukhlas (Mukhlas): Born 2 February 1960 in Lamongan, East Java. Real name Huda bin Abdul Haq, also known as Ali Ghufron. Eldest brother of convicted JI operatives Amrozi and Imron. Became head of the radical Luqmanul Hakiem Islamic School (LHIS) in Johor, Malaysia. On 8 November 2008 he was executed for his role in the Bali One bombing. Just one of many murders he was responsible for.

Ali Amrozi (Amrozi): Born 5 July 1962. Real name Ali Amrozi bin Haji Nurhasyim. Brother of JI operatives Mukhlas and Imron. Became known during the Bali One trials as the smiling assassin. Executed for his role in the Bali One bombing on 9 November 2008.

Ali Imron (Imron): Born 1970. Real name Ali Imron bin Nurhasyim. Youngest brother of Mukhlas and Amrozi. On 18 September 2003, he was convicted for his role in the Bali One bombing and sentenced to life imprisonment. He says he's remorseful for his actions.

Noor din bin Mohammed Top (Top): Born 11 August 1968 in Johor, Malaysia. He was one of Azhari's students at the University of Technology in Malaysia and became Azhari's protege. In September 2009, he was killed by Detachment 88 officers during a raid in Semarang.

Imam Samudra (Samudra): Born 14 January 1970, West Java, Indonesia. Real name Abdul Aziz bin Sihabudin, also known as Hendri, Heri, Fathi, Alfatih and Kudama. Executed for his role in the Bali One bombing on 9 November 2008.

Idris: Also known as Jhoni Hendrawan and al-Gembrot, Idris escaped conviction for his involvement in the 2002 Bali bombing when Indonesia's constitutional court found he could not be convicted on laws passed after that bombing. He was convicted for his involvement with the JW Marriot Hotel bombing and sentenced to 10 years. He was released from prison in 2009 after serving five years.

MAIN EVENTS

24 December 2000 Christmas Eve church bombings;
47 churches and homes of Christian clergymen,
Indonesia.

12 October 2002 Bali One bombings; Paddy's Pub and
the Sari Club, Bali, Indonesia.

5 August 2003 JW Marriott Hotel bombing, Jakarta,
Indonesia.

9 September 2004 Australian embassy bombing, Jakarta,
Indonesia.

1 October 2005 Bali Two bombings; Raja's, Nyoman
and Menega restaurants, Bali, Indonesia.

9 November 2005 Azhari/police shoot-out in Batu,
Malang, Indonesia.

ENDNOTES

1   Terry Fitzgerald, *A Beautiful Boy*, self-published, 2008.

2   Based on an interview between the author and Terry Fitzgerald.

3   Terry Fitzgerald, *A Beautiful Boy*, self-published, 2008.

4   Cholili will later tell several people that he was with Azhari in Batu Malang on the night of the bombing and they heard the news of the bombing on BBC radio. This may have been to avoid police questions about how the three suicide bombers, Azhari and himself eluded Bali's security measures.

5   Ian Munro, Gary Tippet, Lindsay Murdoch and Catherine Munro, 'Killing is never OK', *The Age*, 8 October 2005.

6   Critically injured Australians evacuated to Singapore included Bruce Williamson, Paul John Anicich, Penelope Gladys Anicich, Terry Fitzgerald and Jessica Fitzgerald. Injured Australians evacuated to Darwin included Anthony Purkiss, Maryanne Purkiss, Eric Pilar, Jenny Pilar, Jenny Scott, Nicolas Scott, George Drake, Aleta Lederwasch, Kim Griffiths and Vicki Griffiths. *Herald Sun*, 4 October 2005. Numbers of injured were 64 Indonesians, 20 Australians, 7 South Koreans, 4 Americans, 3 Japanese, 1 French and 1 German. Marian Carroll, 'Bomb went off "under our table"', *The Age*, 3 October 2005.

7   Including but not limited to, Christmas Eve 2000 attacks (and subsequent executions); Sari Club and Paddy's Pub bombings, Bali, 2002; Lippo Bank robbery, Medan 2003; JW Marriot Hotel bombing, Jakarta, 2003; Australian embassy bombing, Jakarta, 2004; Raja's, Menega and Nyoman restaurants bombing, Bali, 2005.

8   For legal reasons these conversations are not directly quoted. They are a representation of the character of what occurred, simplified for the purposes of storytelling.

9   The building referred to is the previous AFP headquarters building in Civic, not the current AFP headquarters location on Kings Avenue, Barton, Canberra. The marking, handling procedures and storage in vaults and strongrooms of top secret classified information can be found in the Australian Government Information Security Management Guidelines,

ENDNOTES

the Australian Government website, and State and Territory Government Security Management Guidelines: www.defence.gov.au; www.protectivesecurity.gov.au; www.finance.gov.au.

10 I have not divulged any currently classified or privileged information, as at February 2017, in this book. Some information that was classified during, and for some time after the bombing investigation in 2005, has subsequently been brought into the public domain by Australian and overseas publications and websites.

11 Sungkar was born on Solo, Central Java, on an unknown date in 1937.

12 Bashir was born on 17 August 1938 in Jombang Regency, Indonesia.

13 *Pesantren* are also called Pondok Pesantren or Madrassa Islamia in some countries.

14 Eric Ellis, 'Why they hate us', *The Bulletin*, 15 September 2004.

15 'Sharia Law Explained', see: www.thereligionofpeace.com and www.billionbibles.org/Sharia/Sharia-law.htm

16 'The Travails of Ngruki Two', *Tempo Magazine*, November 2002.

17 Mukhlas was born Huda bin Abdul Haq aka Ali Ghufron (2 February 1960) in Lamongan, East Java. Amrozi aka Ali Amrozi bin Haji Nurhasyim was born 5 July 1962. Some records indicate that Ali Imron bin Nurhasyim, born in 1970, may have also attended the LHIS in Johor, Malaysia. Separately, Mukhlas and Imron fought and trained in Afghanistan.

18 The hearing was in relation to their earlier successful appeal, which had their sentences reduced to time served.

19 *Gambaran Pena Abu Bakar Ba'asyir*, Baden Intelijen Negara (Indonesian Intelligence – BIN) document in: *The Second Front: Inside Jemaah Islamiyah, Asia's Most Dangerous Terrorist Network*, Ken Conboy, Equinox Publishing, Sheffield, 2006.

20 Azhari was born on 14 September 1957 in Malacca, 150 kms south of Kuala Lumpur, Malaysia.

21 John Cooper, academic at the University of Technology in Malaysia, quoted in 'Dr Azahari Husin – From Fun Bloke Two Murderous Terrorist', 11 November 2005. www.formermuslimsunited.org.

22 The Oxford dictionary describes the noun 'Islamofascist' as, 'A person adhering to a form of Islam perceived as authoritarian or intolerant; a Muslim extremist or fundamentalist.' https://en.oxforddictionaries.com/definition/islamofascist, 30 January 2017.

23 http://www.biography.com/people/ayatollah-ruhollah-khomeini-13680544#political-and-religious-leader

24 Ken Conboy, *The Second Front: Inside Jemaah Islamiyah, Asia's Most Dangerous Terrorist Network*, Equinox Publishing, Sheffield, 2006.

25 Celebrating the end of Ramadan.

26 This type of ill-conceived and out-of-context rhetoric was often used by Islamic fundamentalists to radicalise and inspire others to violence –

DEFEATING TERROR

completely ignoring the scripture encouraging peace and compassion. E.g. Pakistani jihad leader Beitullah Mehsud claims that 'Allah on 480 occasions in the Holy Koran extols Muslims to wage jihad.' in Robert Spencer, Regnery Publishing, Washington DC, 2009. *Complete Infidel's Guide to the Koran*.

27 There are some that doubt Mukhlas's claim that he met Osama bin Laden or saw any conflict. According to Nasir Abas in his book (*Membonka Jamaah Islamiya Pengakuan Mantan Anggoto*) Indonesian students made shallow forays during the late 90s into Afghanistan for field exercises, but did not come into contact with Soviet forces.

28 Hambali was also known as Riduan Isamuddin.

29 Mukhlas married Nasir Abas's sister.

30 Also known as Ali Amrozi bin Haji Nurhasyim.

31 There is some conjecture about the year of birth, ranging from 1991 to 1998.

32 Interview with Scott Butler, 18 March 2005 in Ken Conboy, *The Second Front: Inside Jemaah Islamiyah, Asia's Most Dangerous Terrorist Network*, Equinox Publishing, Sheffield, 2006.

33 Rizal Husen, *Tracing the Footsteps of Dr. Azhari; Most Wanted Fugitive in Indonesia*, Indonesian publication, 2005.

34 Badan Intelijen Negara (Indonesian Intelligence document) *Surat Pernyatataan: Faiz bin Abu Baker Bafana*, 22 October 2002 in *The Second Front: Inside Jemaah Islamiyah, Asia's Most Dangerous Terrorist Network*, Ken Conboy, 2006. The exact wording of the oath that Azhari took is unknown as there are numerous versions of the JI oath.

35 Research papers included: 'Modelling and Rentals for Residential Properties', 'A Guide to an Objective Neighbourhood Assessment', 'Information Technology and Real Estate', 'Office Market Cycle', 'Geographic Information Systems and Analysis' and 'The Real Estate Market'.

36 Raymond Ibrahim, *The Meaning Behind Muslim Beards*, 12 September 2011. The article in www.formermuslimsunited.org states 'because Mohammed wanted his Muslims to look different from infidel Christians and Jews, he ordered them to, "trim closely the moustache and grow the beard." Accordingly, all Sunni schools of law maintain it is forbidden, a "major sin", for men to shave their beards – unless, of course, it is part of a stratagem against the infidel in which case it is permissible.'

37 Hamidon Abdul Ghani stated, 'I can not believe he is a terrorist. He always taught us to be a good person. There is no indication that he was involved in terrorist activities. He never showed that he was an extremist. 'Azahari Buried Near Mother', *TEMPO Interactive*, 17 November 2005.

38 Rizal Husen, *Tracing the Footsteps of Dr. Azhari; Most Wanted Fugitive in Indonesia,* Indonesian publication, 2005.

ENDNOTES

39 Militant Muslim groups such as Abu Sayyaf and the Moro Liberation Front. MILF was created when it split from the Moro Liberation Front in 1977.

40 Rizal Husen, *Tracing the Footsteps of Dr. Azhari; Most Wanted Fugitive in Indonesia*, Indonesian publication, 2005. Statement by unnamed INP spokesman.

41 Quoted in Solahudin and D McRae, *The Roots of Terrorism in Indonesia*, Cornell University Press, Ithaca, NY, 2013.

42 Marian Carroll, 'Bomb went off "under our table"', *The Age*, 3 October 2005.

43 'Travellers contradict report there was no bomb warning', *The Australian*, 4 October 2005.

44 Marian Carroll, 'Future fears messages warn of more attacks', *The Age*, 4 October 2005.

45 Mark Forbes, Michelle Grattan and Brendan Nicholson, 'PM urges Indonesia to ban JI', *The Age*, 4 October 2005.

46 Identification of Amrozi via the L300 van on 3 November 2002.

47 Sixty-five were successfully prosecuted.

48 'Top secret – five eyes' has now been superseded in the Australian Information Security Management Guidelines. See www.gov.au websites. I have not divulged any classified or privileged information in this book. All information is the result of my personal research since leaving the AFP and has been sourced from publicly available websites and literature in English and other languages or has been fictionalised for legal reasons.

49 Imam Samudra also known as Abdul Aziz was born in West Java, Indonesia.

50 Idris al-Gembrot aka Jhoni Hendrawan.

51 The USS *Cole* was attacked in the Yemeni Port of Aden on 12 October 2000.

52 Samudra titled the small team *Tentara Islam Batalyon Badar* (TIBB – Badar Battalion Islamic Army).

53 Estimation based on exploded and unexploded devices in Indonesia, Singapore and Malaysia.

54 Lum Chih Feng, 'Dr Azhari; from Manchester to Jemaah Islamiyah', *Star Online*, 12 November 2005.

55 According to Solahudin and D McRae, *The Roots of Terrorism in Indonesia*, Cornell University Press, Ithaca, NY, 2013, these 'Majelis Qiyadah Mantiqi' were administered by the Amir Jema'ah (most senior leader of Jamaah Islamiyah) through the Central Leadership Council (Majelis Qiyadah Markaziah), the Consultative Assembly, the Fatwa Council and the Internal Discipline Council. For conciseness, the organisational structure has been simplified.

56 Hambali travelled with Al-Qaeda representative Mansour Jabarah. Solahudin and D McRae, *The Roots of Terrorism in Indonesia*, Cornell University Press, Ithaca, NY, 2013.

DEFEATING TERROR

57 Intended targets also included a number of American companies.

58 Australia led the 12,000-strong INTERFET forces that included Bangladesh, Brazil, Canada, Denmark, Egypt, France, Germany, Ireland, Italy, Jordan, Kenya, Malaysia, Norway, Philippines, Portugal, Singapore, South Korea, Thailand and the UK.

59 The tape was released to Al Jazeera in November 2002.

60 The JI footage was widely broadcast in the media in January 2002.

61 Leading bomb-makers included Faturrahman Al Ghozi and Dulmatin.

62 Faturrahman Al Ghozi was the senior JI representative in the Philippines who was to oversee the construction.

63 Based on Nur Aini's own account in Rizal Husen's book *Tracing the Footsteps of Azhari*, translated version. There are some reports in Indonesia that Rizal did not interview Nur Aini as he stated in his book.

64 Based on Nur Aini's own account in Rizal Husen's book *Tracing the Footsteps of Azhari*. The wording of the note has varied in different reports.

65 In addition to this meeting, subsequent planning meetings occurred in southern Thailand and Bangkok – for simplicity in storytelling these have been omitted. A number of other people were present at the February 2002 meeting, such as Mohammed Mansour Jabarah (Canadian), Wan Min bin Wan Mat (Malaysian) and Zilkepli bin Marzuki (Malaysian).

66 The false passport was purchased from Indonesian immigration officials at Tanjung Pinang.

67 Wan Min bin Wan Mat, was nominated as the bagman, who would subsequently transfer cash from Hambali to Mukhlas to fund the Bali One bombings.

68 Keith Moor, '*Insight* editor Keith Moor reconstructs the story behind the 2002 Bali bombings', *Herald Sun*, 7 October 2012. This payment was made up of $6000 USD, $17,000 Singapore and 15,000 rupees.

69 Dulmatin was also known as Amar Usman.

70 The L300 van purchased from Aswar Prianto in East Java for 32 million ruppiah.

71 Also a meeting occurred on 6 October when Abdul Ghani and Umar Kecil were present. There were several other people involved and other locations used for housing participants, holding meetings and bomb/vehicle construction. For simplicity in storytelling a number of these people and places have been excluded.

72 Additional people that assisted with the bomb construction included Umar Patek, Sarjiyo and Abdul Goni.

73 Iqbal and Jimi were recruited by JI operatives Rauf and Samudra. Jimi was also known as Arnasan and Acong.

74 Various accounts have been translated/mistranslated from the Koran by terrorist groups deliberately to inspire potential martyrs.

258

ENDNOTES

75 Excerpts from Keith Moor, '*Insight* editor Keith Moor reconstructs the story behind the 2002 Bali bombings', *Herald Sun*, 7 October 2012.

76 Pastika, whose full name is I Made Mangku Pastika and who became the governor of Bali in 2009, started work in Bali on Friday 18 October 2002.

77 Estimation made by the author based on the number of mobile phones active in Indonesia at the time.

78 Mohammed Nawawi.

79 Rizal Husen, *Tracing the Footsteps of Dr. Azhari; Most Wanted Fugitive in Indonesia;* Indonesian publication, 2005. Ken Conboy, *The Second Front: Inside Jemaah Islamiyah, Asia's Most Dangerous Terrorist Network*, Equinox Publishing, Sheffield, 2006. Solahudin and D McRae, *The Roots of Terrorism in Indonesia*, Cornell University Press, Ithaca, NY, 2013. Published BIN documents dated 2002.

80 According to the testimony of Mohammed Ikhwan (aliases Ismail and Agus) in Jakarta on 28 January 2004, Hambali relied upon bin Laden's fatwa. Reported in 'Indonesia: the Hotel bombings', International Crisis Group, Policy Briefing, 24 July 2009.

81 The meeting was planned for April 2003.

82 Gungun Rusman Gunawan was later arrested.

83 For simplicity the INP, some local district police, Detachment 88 and Satgas are referred to simply as 'INP' or 'Detachment 88' in this story.

84 '"Densus 88" Indonesia's Heroes or Death Squad?', The Global Quorum, 2016.

85 Also known as Asmar Latinsamin.

86 Ali Soufan, *The Black Banners: Inside the Hunt for Al Qaeda*, WW Norton, New York, 2011; US federal court documents (2014) pertaining to Hambali's detention in Guantanamo Bay.

87 Hambali's wife's name is Noralwizah Lee.

88 Solahudin and D McRae, The *Roots of Terrorism in Indonesia,* Cornell University Press, Ithaca, NY, 2013.

89 Abu Qatada was eventually deported to Jordan from the UK in 2013, after a nearly decade-long legal battle to stay in England. Dominic Cascian, 'Profile: Abu Qatada', BBC News, 26 June 2014.

90 Both names changed.

91 Ratno Lukito, *Legal Pluralism in Indonesia: Bridging the Unbridgeable*, Routledge, New York, 2013. Frederic Volpi, *Political Islam: A Critical Reader*, Routledge, New York, 2011.

92 Hasan, aka Agung.

93 Irun Hidayat was also a prominent recruiter/radicaliser of suicide bombers.

94 Azhari revealed the target was the Australian Embassy in August 2004 at two separate meetings. The two meetings have been combined for storytelling purposes.

DEFEATING TERROR

95 Purchased on 6 August 2004 in Pondok Gede area, using a false name 'Heri Kurniawan'.

96 Published on www.islamic-minbar.com.

97 Michael Radu, *Islamism and Terrorist Groups in Asia*, Mason Crest Publishers, Broomall, PA, USA, 2006.

98 Andrew Leigh and Pierre van der Eng, 'Top Incomes in Indonesia, 1920–2004', Australian National University, Canberra, 2007.

99 Hasan Alisa Purnomo, Ramadni alias Syaiful Bahri and Soghir alias Abdul Fatah.

100 According to US embassy cables from Jakarta in 2006 surrounding the Bali Two trials, the men also used online chatting and instant messaging. See wikileaks.org.

101 Also known as Reno/Tedy/Tedi. wikileaks.org.

102 Based on the 'Bali Planning Document', later recovered from Azhari's bomb factory in Batu, Malang. Published in *Tempo* magazine, November 2005. See also Raymond Bonner, 'A terror strike, choreographed on a computer', *The New York Times*, 3 July 2006.

103 The villa was located at Block L9 of Perumahan Flamboyan Indah, Kota Batu, Malang.

104 Anif Solchanudin.

105 This document would eventually be recovered by law enforcement following Azhari's death.

106 Salik Firdaus from Majalengka, West Java; Misno from Cilacap, Central Java; Aip Hidyat from Ciamis, West Java; and Anif Solchanudin from Semerang, Central Java.

107 Photographs appeared in the media on 3 October 2005.

108 For legal reasons, I've changed the circumstances of where the note was located, its content and some of its characteristics.

109 Conversation changed. Indonesian and other news sites later published details of a plan found in Azhari's computer to bomb the Bali memorial. A WordPress blog published specific details of this plan, which (translated) states, '... a terror plot in Azhari's computer also contains a plan for three bomb blasts yet to materialise. One: suicide bomber using a small backpack bomb to blow up the monument to the Bali bombings that killed 202 people, including 88 Australians; Two: bombing the Ubud art market, and; Three: bombing Kuta Beach, where foreign tourists sunbathe and enjoy the beach.' https://tidakmenarik.wordpress.com/2009/07/27/inilah-skrenario-bom-di-komputer-dr-azahari/

On 4 October 2005, a federal government spokesman was quoted as saying 'no decision had been made to cancel the ceremony, but the situation was under review'. The Foreign Affairs Department is quoted as issuing a fresh travel warning, saying 'the risk of an attack in Bali is heightened because of the approaching anniversary. The possibility of another attack

ENDNOTES

against Australians cannot be ruled out'. Mark Coorey, 'Review of plans to mark 2002 tragedy', *Adelaide Advertiser,* 4 October 2005.

110   Tsanawiyah Madrasah, Cikijing; Darussa'dah Boyolali *Pesantren.*

111   The real content of the conversation and the identity of the person remain classified. As such, I have modified both for legal reasons.

112   Name changed.

113   Ian McPhedran and Nick Butterly, 'Bio-terror hits embassy', *The Courtier Mail,* 2 June 2005.

114   ibid.

115   Kim Landers, 'Investigation underway into embassy powder scare', ABC Online, 2 June 2005. During the interview Alexander Downer stated 'The Indonesian police have agreed to provide some officers to assist this investigation. Three Indonesian national police members and one representative from the Indonesian Ministry of Agriculture will travel to Canberra to form part of the joint investigation team.' Conversation modified for legal reasons.

116   Name changed.

117   Names changed.

118   Kim Landers, 'Investigation underway into embassy powder scare', ABC Online, 2 June 2005.

119   Copies of item were brought to the Forward Command Post, originals were retained by the INP. Other INP officers were also involved but have been excluded for simplicity.

120   Ayip Hidayat was later confirmed as the Raja's bomber.

121   'Bali 11 Trials Progress, Experienced Terrorism Prosecutor Leads the Way', Public Library of US Diplomacy, 6 July 2006. https://wikileaks.org.

122   Ridwan Max Sijabat and Indra Hasaputra, 'Azhari in touch with family while on the run', *Jakarta Post,* 15 November 2005.

123   Conversation modified.

124   Deborah Snow, 'Federal police take softly-softly approach in helping Indonesian colleagues', *The Sydney Morning Herald,* 11 November 2005.

125   'Australia welcomes Azhari's reported death in gunfight', 11 November 2005, Agence France-Presse, Sydney, Australia.

126   Article by Indonesia correspondent Mark Forbes, 18 November 2005.

127   Also known as Wiwid, Sigit and Bambang Bin Pramono, born 9 February 1972.

128   Also known as Ja'far, born 16 September 1975.

129   For the safety of the people I interviewed, who could otherwise be targeted by JI members, I've maintained their anonymity.

130   *Koran* 47:4 Translation by N J Dawood, *The Koran*, Penguin, London 2014.

131   In most Muslim-majority countries, atheists are afforded less legal protection than other non-Muslim faiths. For example, in Indonesia, citizens must believe in one of six declared religions; atheism and

agnosticism are excluded. Similarly, Egypt's constitution allows only three religions: Christianity, Judaism and Islam. The Economist article 'No God, Not Even Allah' (24 November 2012) states that sharia law assumes people are born into their parents' religion, 'Thus ex-Muslim atheists are guilty of apostasy – a *hudud* crime against God, like adultery and drinking alcohol. Potential sanctions can be severe: eight states, including Iran, Saudi Arabia, Mauritania and Sudan have the death penalty on their statute books for such offences.'

132 John Cooper, academic at the University of Technology in Malaysia, quoted in *Dr Azahari Husin – From Fun Bloke To Murderous Terrorist*, 11 November 2005.

133 Neelima Choahan with Adam Cooper and Nick Miller, 'Sevdet Besim, 19, gets 10 years' jail for Anzac Day plot to behead police officer', *The Age*, 5 September 2016.

134 List of Terrorist Attacks 1981 to 2009. List of Islamic Terrorist Attacks (Volume 2) Pedia Press https://pediapress.com.

135 Ex-Muslim Brother Rasheed on http://www.islamexplained.com.

136 Ryan Emery, 'A West Australian church has opened its doors and hearts to include Muslim parishioners in its community', SBS, 20 November 2016.

About the Author

David Craig served with the Australian Federal Police (AFP) for 22 years, for the last 10 years at the rank of Detective Superintendent. He completed a doctorate in law (covert operations) in 2001. He was a founding member of the AFP international undercover program and trained with the Royal Canadian Mounted Police and the FBI. He served with the United Nations in East Timor and was deployed to Afghanistan, where he was based with Australian troops in Tarin Kowt and Kandahar. He retired from the AFP in 2013 and now resides in Sydney, Australia.